Time Out For Tired Moms

finally Mom, go to your room!

Time -Out

For Tired Moms

finally Mom,

go to your room!

Judy Crawford

AMBASSADOR INTERNATIONAL
GREENVILLE, SOUTH CAROLINA & BELFAST, NORTHERN IRELAND

TIME OUT FOR TIRED MOMS
finally Mom, go to your room!

All unmarked Scriptures are taken from the Holy Bible, NEW INTERNA-
TIONAL VERSION®. Copyright © 1973, 1978, 1984 International Bible
Society. All rights reserved throughout the world. Used by permission of
International Bible Society.

Marked Scriptures are taken from The Message. Copyright © 1993, 1994,
1995, 1996, 2000, 2001, 2002. Used by permission of NavPress Publishing
Group.

Cover design and page layout by David Siglin of A&E Media

ISBN 978-1-932307-88-7

Published by the Ambassador Group

Ambassador International
427 Wade Hampton Blvd.
Greenville, SC 29609
USA
www.emeraldhouse.com

and

Ambassador Publications Ltd.
Providence House
Ardenlee Street
Belfast BT6 8QJ
Northern Ireland
www.ambassador-productions.com

The colophon is a trademark of Ambassador

Dedication

To Gary, the love of my life

And my children, Michaela, Adam, Will and Joseph

You are my inspiration!

Without you, there wouldn't be a book!

Acknowledgements

Many thanks goes to:

My husband Gary. You are a patient man. I love you babe!

My kids, Michaela, Adam, Will, and Joseph. What can I say...You are the best!

My parents for always telling me I was wonderful, even when I knew better.

Laura Bowles and Pam Crawford. Your encouraging critiques helped get me started.

Dr. Jim Hill. Your sermons inspired many of these stories. Thanks!

My M.I.L.K. Moms. This book is for you! Thank you for your prayers and support!

Susan Burns, my sister in Christ, your prayers mean a lot!

My Mother-in-law, Dorothy Crawford. Thank you for your willingness to always help with the kids so I could pursue this dream.

All my friends and family that have prayed me through the writing of this book.

Sam Lowry, David Siglin and everyone at Ambassador International. Thank you for giving a rookie a chance and your excellence in publishing Christian literature.

Finally, I need to thank God, my Lord and Savior, Jesus Christ. You are my all in all. Thank you for the Yes! I have finally finished the work. I pray that You will use it for Your Glory.

Table of Contents

Introduction

Time-outs have always been my favorite form of discipline. Whenever sibling rivalries flare, a quick, "Go to your rooms!" is a sure fix to the problem. Something magical happens in those few minutes of isolation. Tempers cool. Attitudes change. A renewing occurs when they are separated from the situation. When my kids are finally released, they always have a smile on their faces, a hug to offer, and a better outlook on life. One day, the question proposed itself, "When do Moms get Time-Outs?" We need space, time for introspection, time to refocus, and maybe even time to vent a little. We need time-out too!

Let's face it, Mothering is hard. Moms everywhere are tired. We're tired of laundry, tired of multi-tasking, tired of the boys belching in the backseat of the minivan. Did I mention laundry? Yes, we're tired!

As I faithfully cheer my Little League sons from the side lines, I can't help but notice the similarities between wild pitches and Mothering. You see, the art of Mothering is much like stepping up to bat at the dusty plate of parenting. Every ball thrown at you is a curve ball from a different direction and things can often get quite dangerous really fast.

One day I thought I would jot down a few of the curve balls thrown my way.

1. I never thought I would have to instruct my son that the oven is not a good place to hide. I've heard of people hiding dirty dishes there, even stacks of mail—but little boys?! I don't think so.

2. I never thought I would have to teach my children that rinsing their toothbrushes out in the toilet is not good hygiene. Just the thought, is soooo disgusting.

3. I never thought I would have to educate my son that bird baths are for birds to bathe in, not for little boys to potty in. He really did this—at my sister's church. UGH!

Last summer, I was strolling through my dining room when I happened upon an unwrapped tootsie roll on the floor. A wash of irritation swept over me. *How many times have I told the kids to hit the trash can, and why is there candy on the floor anyway? Don't they know it's almost dinner time?* You know the routine. Anyway, as I bent down to pick it up, its unique texture immediately became apparent. It wasn't a tootsie roll at all. It was a gift from my potty training toddler, a trail of bread crumbs he had left behind on his way to the bathroom and even worse, it was in my hand. YUCK!

Yes, I believe I can safely say that today's Moms are tired. Our children drain us both mentally and physically. Please, send us to our rooms. (Can you feel my pain?)

Here are a few tell-tale signs that you are a Mother that desperately needs some time-out.

1. When you catch yourself tossing suckers over your shoulder in an attempt to quiet the savage beasts in the back of your minivan…you probably need some time-out.

2. When you give up the chase and reason that your toddler's naked bottom could use some airing out anyway…it's likely that you need time-out.

3. When your vision becomes blurred enough to see the smudgy hand prints that litter your walls as décor accents…it is definitely a sign that you need time-out.

Yes, tired Moms everywhere need time-out. We need time to refocus and seek God's insight on how to better tackle that two-year-old or rather the problems we're having with our two-year-old. We need to know that we're not alone in this battle. Even if other Moms abandon you, and they will if your kid is coughing too much; God is there. He is as close as that pea your child just shot across the kitchen table.

Did you know that God understands a Mother's frustrations? He understands our need to find moments of peace in our lives. I'm sure many of you are familiar with the popular initials WWJD, a.k.a. "What would Jesus Do?" One day, I thought I would check it out. What did Jesus do? So I looked it up. Guess what? Over and over as I perused my Bible I came across recorded accounts of Jesus going off to a quiet place all by himself to do what, to seek time-out. Just like today's modern Mom, Jesus too needed time to renew his spirit, time to refocus, and seek God's insight... and He did.

The interesting thing is, when Jesus sought time-out...space if you will...just a few peaceful moments without anyone vying for his attention (O.K. I'll stop. You get the point) what do you think happened next? Well, let's take a look. Matthew 14:13 reads, "When Jesus heard what had happened, he withdrew by boat privately to a solitary place. Hearing of this, the crowds followed him on foot from the towns." Did you get that? You don't have to read between the lines. It is right there in black and white. Read it again, "...the crowds followed..." Yes, they followed! All He wanted was a few quiet minutes alone and the people had the gall to interrupt his solitude. (Can you relate?) Not only did they follow, they wanted something from Him. They were needy. They wanted to be healed, to be fed. (Sound familiar?) Yes, Jesus kissed boo-boos and served fishy crackers much like modern Moms do today.

Jesus really *does* understand a Mother's dilemma. He understands when you lock yourself in the bathroom for just a few minutes of "fresh air" only to discover tiny wiggly fingers under the crack in the door seeking your attention. (Really, why do children do this anyway? Do they actually think they can somehow make it through?) Jesus understands, because he has walked in your shoes. Well, maybe fuzzy pink slippers weren't his accustomed attire. But, he did journey down a similar path. He too had people constantly groping for his undivided attention.

The amazing thing was, when Christ sought time-out... and was followed, His response was always the same. His response was always compassion. Let's take another peak. Matthew 14:14 continues, "When Jesus landed and saw a large crowd, he had compassion on them and healed their sick." Isn't that utterly incredible! He had compassion! Compassion!!! Reality check! Is our response always compassion? Unfortunately, mine is not. I can't say that I have always been that Christ-like. My friends, that is exactly why Moms need time-out. So we don't go there. We want to turn the stove down before the pot boils over.

Time-out makes a Mom more flexible. When you boil spaghetti its very essence shifts from hard to soft. It becomes supple and appealing. Moms need to go through a similar transition. Sometimes all we need is a good hot soak, a long luxurious bubble bath, to de-stress and do just that.

We need to be more like Jesus. We need to seek time-out so that we can have that compassionate response that Jesus did. That in essence is what time-out is all about. It's a shift in attitude. It is more than just counting to ten or one hundred if needed. And its definition is much broader than "*Calgone* take me away."

For the sake of this book, my definition of a time-out is: *A time-out is anything that lifts your spirits and adjusts your attitude in a positive way.* We are headed south and need to be turned back north again. Isn't that why we send our children to their rooms in the first place? We send them there to properly adjust their attitudes. Their attitude has shifted in the wrong direction and it needs a little adjusting to take that 180 degree turn back to where it should be. By keeping ourselves in check we can avoid some of the pitfalls that many of us fall into, feelings of being overwhelmed, angry outbursts or depression are all real consequences that might occur when time-out is neglected. We want to pull the weeds of discontentment in our lives before they get out of hand so we can reap a harvest of peace, contentment, and yes, compassion. Just like Jesus.

That is why Time-Out for Tired Moms was written. Each week of this eight week devotional begins with a Time-Out Tip category. As you read through the multitude of creative time-out suggestions take note of how you can incorporate them into your day to day life as a Mother. Each Time-Out Tip category is then followed by five daily devotions to help you reconnect with God the true refresher of a Mother's soul. Together, its dual purpose is meant to give you the respite you rightfully deserve; so your response to frustrating Mommy moments will always be the Christ-like compassion that Jesus demonstrated.

One additional note, it is vitally important that *Time-Out for Tired Moms* directs Bible study. It is not intended to be a substitute. That is why *Time for Teaching* scriptures are referenced instead of quoted. So *The* Book, the Bible will be opened. It is the most important read of your day.

Well Mom, it is time to begin. It is my prayer that your soul will be refreshed...your attitude properly adjusted...your response always Christ-like compassion. So, sit back and enjoy. Today, it is finally *your turn* to GO TO YOUR ROOM!

Nurture Your Spirit

After leaving them, he went up on a mountainside to pray.
Mark 6:46

Time-Out to nurture your spirit is the perfect place to start. Do you have a quiet time or rather a *less* quiet time each day in which you read your Bible and pray? "When do I find time?" asks the frazzled Mom with a toddler on her hip, a basket of laundry permanently attached to the other as a second child wraps himself around the safe haven of Mommy's leg in an attempt to hide from an older sibling's pestering. I identify with that frazzled Mom's predicament because that Mom is me. For years I struggled to find a peaceful moment with God. As days went by without a "quiet time," guilt set in. Finally, I'd kneel before God in repentance and vow to never let my to-do list and kids come between us again only to fail once more just days later.

Mom, Jesus understands your dilemma. Remember, the people followed, they constantly groped for His attention, just like our kids do to us. But, that didn't sway Him. Jesus still found time to connect with God through prayer even though He *was* God. He was persistent. We need to be determined too.

If a quiet time-out with God is not a standard part of your day, this is a great place to start. With His divine touch working in your life, you can find peace and joy even in the busiest most stressful Mommy moments. When you have that relationship and nurture it every day, God equips you for the challenge. He shoulders the load, making the burden lighter, bearable, even doable. With God on your side, your response to all of those crazy kid encounters will be that Christ-like compassion that we so desperately desire to emulate.

I believe God designs each of us with a hole in our heart, a space that can only be filled by Him. We try to fill that round hole with lots of square pegs: money, stuff, food, busyness…are just a few. If only we would realize and accept that the deep yearning in our souls is really our innate desire to know God and then fill it with Him, we would find the peace, contentment, and joy that we so long for. I've had times when I walked with God; times I've purposely walked away from God in rebellion, and times that He has carried me through. You can try to walk away from God and say that you don't need Him, but that doesn't change the fact that He is still there and loves you regardless.

God loves you, yes you, the Mom with a load of laundry permanently attached to one hip and a crabby little one balanced on the other and His passionate desire is to develop a deep abiding love relationship with you. But to do that, it takes time. Allow God to shoulder your burden, carry your load, or at least relieve one hip. Take time-out for God, time-out to nurture your spirit and enjoy the richest blessing of all.

TIME OUT TIPS

Find a prayer partner! I have a close friend I meet with once a week to pray. We keep each other accountable while encouraging our Mothering efforts. Ladies, God honors prayer, and He does respond. Boldly ask a friend to be your prayer partner and then commit to meet on a regular basis.

Keep a prayer notebook! When my friend and I meet, we keep a record of prayer concerns by jotting down requests in a little notebook. Answered prayers are highlighted as a reminder that God is listening.

Make a prayer flip book! I write down prayer requests on index cards and then organize them in a small inexpensive photo album. This flip book keeps my prayer time focused and helps me remember specific prayer requests.

Write in a prayer journal! Take a few minutes to write your prayers down in a journal. Write for yourself and don't worry about being prolific. That's not the point. Pour your heart out to God through the written word and then keep your journals as a reminder of God's awesome faithfulness.

Organize a devotional basket! Equip a small basket with a few quiet time supplies so you can quickly take advantage of those rare moments when the kids are quietly entertaining themselves. I suggest stocking your basket with a devotional book (*Time-Out for Tired Moms*) or magazine, highlighter, pen, prayer journal, tissues, note cards, and your Bible of course.

Make memory verse cards! Write or create computer printed note cards of your favorite scripture verses and then place them strategically around the house to memorize. I have a little note card stand on the shelf above my kitchen sink. As I wash dishes, I am also cleaning out my heart and mind by memorizing God's Word. Organize them in a small photo album to take with you when you are on-the-go.

Kneel when you pray! There is something about kneeling in submission to God that helps focus the mind when praying. I like to kneel by my bed and pray. (I make sure my bed is made first.)

Take advantage of little minutes! Don't feel defeated if you don't have a free hour to pray each day. You can still stay connected with God by taking advantage of little minutes. Ten minutes here and there of sincere prayer throughout the day works wonders. Become aware of opportunities to spend short time slots with God and then do it.

Set a time and place! Work into your schedule a set time and place each day to meet with God and then guard it from distractions.

Pray without ceasing! If a time alone with God is not an option because of the constant demands of little ones, learn to develop an attitude of prayer throughout the day. Tie in the theme of your prayers with the task at hand. Ask God to wash your sins as white as snow as you add bleach to your laundry whites. Pray for each child as you sort and fold their clothes. When God brings someone to mind, pray for them right then. Pray without ceasing, and experience God's joy in the everydayness of your life.

Join a Bible study! We are so blessed to have a wide assortment of wonderful Bible study resources available to us. Join a group or start one, choose and obtain materials, and then set a schedule.

God is the ultimate time-out attitude adjuster. Over the next eight weeks as you read *Time-Out for Tired Moms*, commit some time each day to pray and study God's Word. Jesus did and you can too!

DAY 1

Choosing the Best

*...but only one thing is needed. Mary has chosen what is better, and
it will not be taken away from her.* Luke 10:42

The drudgery of washing the morning dishes seemed to drag
on and on. Reaching for the final few, I hesitated sensing trouble was brewing. Glancing over my shoulder, I caught a quick
glimpse of the culprit peering out from behind the bedroom
door. As our eyes locked his baby blues widened with surprise.
Startled, he jerked the door shut. His curiosity, however, caught
the best of him as he cracked the door open again. Catching
his glance a second time, I teased from across the room. Slam,
caught again! Back and forth we played our little game of peek-
a-boo until finally he burst forth with a full throttle trot to greet
me. Quickly drying my hands, I bent down to catch his embrace.
Just as I leaned forward to brace myself for the impact, his sassy
smile exploded into giggles and he darted to the right. Flopping
forward, I let out a heavy sigh of disappointment. I really needed
that hug today.

Joseph's sidetracking tendencies are so frustrating. Just about
anything can suck his attention away from where I want it to be.
Then again, the apple doesn't fall far from the tree? Sidetracking
is my life. It seems that I spend most days jumping from one task
to the next, never really accomplishing much of anything.

Looking up from my sink full of suds, I spotted my Bible ly-
ing open on the kitchen table. I had every intention of spending
some time in the Word today, but once again the tyranny of the
urgent won. There always seems to be so much to do in so little
time. I have a Martha nature when what I really need is a Mary
heart.

When Martha complained to Jesus that Mary wasn't cutting
it in the kitchen, He gently rebuked, "Martha, Martha, you are
worried and upset about many things, but only one thing is need-

ed. Mary has chosen what is better, and it will not be taken away from her." (Luke 10:41-42) I can just imagine Martha catching the lump in her throat as the sting of His accusation sunk in. A tidal wave of questions may have flooded her mind. *Doesn't He understand? Doesn't He care? Preparations must be made!* On and on good things pulled her away from the one thing.

Martha wanted to please through service. But, was the extravagance really necessary? What was the real point of this unexpected visit? Instead of running to the feet of Jesus, she allowed good things to distract her and missed out on the *hug* that Mary had chosen.

Every morning I wake up with good intentions. God is waiting in the living room of my heart anticipating my morning embrace. Instead I allow kitchen duties to sidetrack me from my divine appointment. Then I reason that I best start a load of laundry. Next thing I know it's time to prepare lunch. The one thing gets lost in the sea of need-to-dos. Why it is so hard to choose what is better?

Putting away those final dishes, my body jolted as Joseph finally connected with that promised hug around my knees. "There you are!" I bent down to return the embrace. Smothering him with affection he finally broke free and darted off once again. Standing up my eyes once again caught sight of that open Bible beaconing me. With a new resolve, I set my dishrag aside. I needed another hug today. The laundry would have to wait. One thing is all that is really needed and today I choose the best.

TIME FOR HIM

Dear Lord, my heart's desire is to know You. Forgive me when I let other things distract me. Help me to better prioritize my time. Give me a heart that seeks You first.

TIME FOR MOM

Mothers tend to be masters at multi-tasking. There is never just one thing on our to-do list. Our days are littered with a variety of duties that all need to be done now—right now! Or so it seems. Do we ever find time to sit at His feet? When do we focus on the one thing and momentarily let everything else go?

This is the type of devotion I feel that God really desires from us. Popcorn prayers, those spur of the moment requests, have their place. But we need to find time—make time—schedule time to meet with our heavenly Father one on one every day.

I struggle with this as I'm sure many of you do. Kids can be so demanding of our attention. But we can't use our children as an excuse. Instead we need a little attitude adjustment.

It's really not about us making time for God. It's about God making time for us. It's an honor we take all too lightly. It's not that we *need* to take time for God. It's that we *get to.* God has opened up His schedule for us. The least we can do is show up for the appointment.

But, you just don't understand! I have to change the baby, wash the dishes, cart my kids around, then there's that church committee that meets every Tuesday night… Martha, Martha, only one thing is needed. Choose what is better!

Don't let the Martha in you allow you to miss out on the better part. Today, keep the appointment. Keep it tomorrow too. I know it's not easy. But, keep it anyway! Keep it again and again until you find that you can't start your day until you've received your heavenly hug. God will bless you for your commitment. Keep the one thing, the *one thing* and experience the best that God has to offer.

TIME FOR TEACHING

Read: Psalm 5:3 and Luke 10:38-42

God wants to meet you every day. Don't let kitchen duties distract you. Keep your focus on the "one thing" and experience God's best.

The Gift of Grace

Grace and peace to you from God our Father and the Lord Jesus Christ.
Philippians 1:2

It had been a long day of shopping. The mutual exasperation between me and my toddler seemed to peak at our last stop. *If only I can get Joseph buckled into his car seat, I will be home free!* I encouraged myself as my stride quickened through the parking lot. Juggling my son and my groceries; I quickly unloaded my cart as it gently came to rest on the vehicle next to mine. I didn't think much of it until its owner suddenly appeared fuming as she approached.

"Why is your cart touching my car?" she barked a prelude to the symphony of complaints that followed. My last nerve had already been stepped on; I really didn't need this—NOW. Hastily unloading my cart, I attempted to politely reason with her to no avail. She was ticked and she made sure I knew it.

Though outwardly I held my tongue, inwardly I let her have it. *Lady, my cart was barely touching your car—but if you would like, I'd love to show you what kind of damage it can really do...* I fantasized as I jerked my cart away from her vehicle, faithfully returned it to the holding bin, and slammed it in to let off a little steam.

When I got back to my car, her mouth still runneth over. Seething myself, I ignored her ranting, got into my van, and stepped on the gas to head home.

Fortunately, Joseph fell asleep, ending one battle while the wounds from the other began to fester. I just couldn't shake it. Or rather, I didn't want to. As I drove home, I relished the thought of what I *could* have done to that rude woman's car. Stopping at the mailbox on my way into the drive I couldn't resist congratulating my *Christian* restraint to her obviously out of line remarks.

Shifting through the mail, I noticed a personal letter, a welcomed diversion from a trying day. Breathing in a moment of quiet, I quickly opened the envelope too eager to wait. To my surprise, it contained an unexpected check. As I read the amount and the note that was attached, a floodgate of tears swept over me.

You see, I had been praying for God to provide funds for an upcoming family vacation. In that envelope was a direct answer to my prayer, a check written specifically to help us pay for our trip. Wow! I was overwhelmed by God's awesome provision.

As waves of emotion continued, a sour unease began to swell as my unworthiness of such a gift at this point in time became apparent. All the way home I had mentally rehearsed how I had wanted to respond to that lady in the parking lot, and it wasn't a pretty picture. Little did I know waiting in my mailbox was God's gift of generosity when I deserved it the least.

"What was my gift to her?" I considered. I may have held my tongue, but my heart wasn't in it. Who knows what excess baggage she might have been carrying that afternoon? Maybe, she was recently diagnosed with cancer, maybe her husband had left her, or maybe she too was just having a bad day and needed a kind word, a shoulder to cry on.

Gifts come in all sorts of packages. Some tucked in crisp white envelopes and some tucked in lessons learned.

Lord, thank You for the gift of grace, and next time help me to offer it as well.

☺ TIME FOR HIM ☺

Gracious God, thank You for blessing me in so many ways even when I deserve it the least. Forgive me when my thoughts and actions fail to honor You. Help me to be every mindful of Your daily grace and equip me to generously follow Your example.

☺ TIME FOR MOM ☺

One day, my young son ran to me screaming in terror as he flailed about in his failed attempts to free a bee that had somehow got caught inside his shirt. Now I have heard that bees can only sting once but the panic in his eyes told me something different. I quickly removed his shirt while making sure the bee remained caught inside its fabric. Immediate relief swept over him as his thoughts unexpectedly shifted away from his own wounds to the fate of the bee.

"What are you going to do with it?" he quizzed.

"I am going to kill it, of course," I curtly remarked, flabbergasted that he even cared.

Then something utterly amazing took place. Without hesitation, he straightened his stance and stated with conviction, "Mom, that bee is one of God's creatures just like me. You shouldn't kill it."

"Shouldn't kill it?!" I questioned. His left field remark caught me completely off guard. My son was just traumatized by this bee and now he wants me to save its life. No way! Besides, has he forgotten his genetic makeup? He's a boy! Boys love to smash things, squish bugs, dissect frogs, shall I continue? That's what boys do. Did the bee sting somehow poison his brain?

As the shock wore off, the authenticity of his concern sunk in and the word grace began to softly resonate within. Grace…a simple word…so hard to give…so overwhelming to receive. Grace.

I am so thankful for God's lavish grace on my life. The sting of my tongue is often much worse than that of a bee. Yet over and over, God forgives and offers the gift of grace…amazing grace…oh, how sweet the sound.[1]

What gift do you offer when you are stung by life or picked on in the parking lot? Do you offer grace? Grace that sees past self into the heart of another and then grants compassion even when it is least deserved. Today, turn the other check. Give what you have so freely received. Bless someone with the gift of grace.

⏱ TIME FOR TEACHING ⏱

Read: Ephesians 2:8, Luke 6:29-31, and Colossians 4:6

The definition of grace is unmerited favor. I am so thankful for God's unmerited favor on my life. Live by His example and give the gift of grace.

DAY 3

The Adventures of a Potty Training Flunky

Teach me to do your will, for you are my God; may your good Spirit lead me on level ground. Psalm 143:10

As I examined the merchandise in front of me, the corner of my eye caught a shift in expression on my young son's face. He was far too serious for an afternoon outing at Wal-Mart. Any half experienced Mother knows that *look*.

Returning my glance, he let out a quiet grunt with the plea, "Potty Mom."

A spark of elation ignited as I questioned his request, "Do you have to go potty Joe?" You see, for him to ask to go potty was a truly novel revelation. We had been working on this concept for over a year and any sliver of advancement down this beaten path, well, just made me want to jump for joy.

Instantly, a rush of urgency jolted me to a high alert code red as I hastily took note of the whereabouts of the closest commode. If my calculations were correct, we just might make it.

With a new burst of energy I thrust the cart forward while instructing Joseph to "Hold on!" as we raced down the aisle breaking all shopping cart speed limits. With no time to spare, we came to an abrupt halt in front of the rest room, and I briskly whisked him out of the cart just as two ladies were exiting.

"Watch out! We have an emergency!" I cautioned. Wisely making way, we rushed passed to the first available stall. Dropping his drawers my euphoria quickly faded as it became apparent that although we did make it for the main event, premature leakage had soiled his underwear, his jeans, and had even run down to his socks. And where was the diaper bag—in the car of course!

I had ridden this roller coaster ride of disappointment so many times before that the thought of cleaning up just one more mess literally made me sick. Bone weary I barked orders for Joseph to "Hold still!" in my futile attempts to clean him up while he proceeded to tee pee our confined quarters with every inch of toilet tissue his little hands could unroll. Struggling to maintain control, I kneeled to rinse his stained Scooby Doos in the toilet when I noticed that this particular toilet had a motion sensor flushing device on it. Uh Oh! We had created quite a mess. A shot of panic ran through my body as I wondered, *"Would it automatically flush when I stood up? I don't know? I haven't recently kneeled to go to the bathroom."* Not wanting to take my chances, I began to sway to and fro in front of the porcelain pot like some sort of odd native tribal toilet flushing ritual.

It was then that it hit me. Maybe it was the out of body glimpse of me dancing in front of the toilet tabernacle while my toddler taunted from behind that did it. I'm not sure. But, the foolishness and futility of it all smacked me in the face with the realization, *"What have I become? I hold a Master's Degree in "education" of all things, and I can't teach my son to poop in the potty. I can't even flush this stupid toilet! I am a mess! I am a washed up potty training flunky! UGH!"*

God has a way of humbling the proud, doesn't He? Just when I thought I had my act all together…just when I thought I had this Mothering thing down pat… God had to throw something like potty training at me to make sure I understood who was really in control. My son!

Actually, as I lift my children up to God with open hands I realize that ultimately He is in control. And by His divine mercy and grace, three out of four of my children do successfully wear underpants. Hope is on the horizon.

Refashioning my son's slightly soiled jeans onto his naked bottom, we made our exit as the triumphant swoosh of the toilet flushing added exclamation to my new found spark of hope. *I guess toilets really do flush when you leave the stall.* The lingering aroma sure made navigating the busy aisles of Wal-Mart so much easier. Just as we were about to finalize our purchases, Joseph's expression sobered as his distressed glance caught my eye once more.

Make way! It's a Code Red! Here we go again…

⏱ TIME FOR HIM ⏱

Lord, You are in control. In Your hands rests the world and all that it contains. Thank You for bearing the burden so I don't have too. Teach me to have a heart that always submits to You.

⏱ TIME FOR MOM ⏱

Christians love to proclaim that God is in control. We sing its praises. We comfort hurting friends with its reassurance. We pray "Thy will be done." Yet as soon as the words escape our lips an internal uneasiness questions their sincerity.

Yes, God is in control. There is no doubt the He set this vast expanse into motion and continues to maintain its ongoing existence. The question is, "Do we acknowledge the fact that God is in control—and we're not?"

Dad may be the head of the household but often Mom is the one that runs it. Reeling all of this power can lead to an over-confident sense that Mom controls everything. We try to micromanage our home and our kids. But our continual failures weigh us down until finally the burden forces us to our knees. It is only from this perspective that we see that God is in control and we don't have to be.

If control freak is a title found on your resume, step down from the position. As hard as you try, you will never control everything. This world is far too complicated, too difficult for any one Mom to manage. Don't be trapped by an attitude that says my way. Instead, say Thy way and free yourself from the burden. Trust God and see for yourself.

⏱ TIME FOR TEACHING ⏱

Read: Psalm 40:8, Acts 21:14, and Matthew 26:42

Even Jesus in the garden of Gethsemane relinquished His will to the Fathers. Should we be any different? Submit yourself to God, and enjoy the calm reassurance that you don't have to do and be it all.

DAY 4

W.O.W.

Delight yourself in the Lord and He will give you the desires of your heart. Psalms 37:4

Glancing at the clock, my heart raced as the nervousness in my eyes connected with my husband across our kitchen table.

"They will announce the winner any minute. Do you really think I have a chance?" I questioned almost unable to contain my excitement.

The day before the manager of our local Christian radio station had called. "I need to ask you a few questions…" he explained while breaking the news that I was a *potential* winner of their most recent contest.

Needless to say, that phone call prompted a plethora of pondering. *How many "potential" winners are there? Do I really have a chance? Could I actually be one of the two names chosen?*

As the clock ticked the tension in the room grew until finally the moment had arrived. Through it all my ears and eyes remained glued to the telephone. As a seasoned listener to this particular station, I knew they would call the winner first in order to break the exciting news live on air. But, the phone never rang and then the winner was announced.

"Oh well." I shrugged to my husband. Realizing that without that telling phone call my chances of winning were zip, I relaxed in my seat while remaining attentive as they announced the winner of the second drawing.

Then it happened! "The winner of our $500.00 shopping spree is JUDY CRAWFORD!"

"WOW!" I screamed. The emotion that followed was a hodgepodge of laughter, tears, and shouts of disbelief. Never before had I won a prize of such magnitude. It felt like I had just won a million dollars! The rest of the day was washed with the warm glow of awe, gratitude, and astonishment.

I have never been one to believe in chance happenings. In fact a favorite quote goes something like this, "Coincidence is when God works a miracle but chooses to remain anonymous." (Author unknown) God works through all circumstances of life, even drawings on the local radio station. You see, the week before I was debating whether or not we could afford the gas to transport my daughter back and forth to participate in a community musical. When you live thirty minutes from town with today's gas prices, this is an issue. The $500.00 shopping spree I won was given to me in the form of a *gas* gift card. Coincidence? I think not. God not only *WOW*ed me, He directly met my need in a big way. The love that simple gift was wrapped in overwhelmed my heart. Wow, says it all.

Last summer, as we were driving along the highway, I noticed a billboard advertising a church. The name of the church was W.O.W. which stood for Walk On Water. The sign struck a chord. A W.O.W. moment is when you look down and realize that you have stepped off into the impossible and God is the only explanation.

I believe God wants to W.O.W. all of us. He wants to bless us and work in our lives in such an awesome way that we can only point up to Him. Isn't that what that verse says, "Delight yourself in the Lord and He will give you the desires of your heart." (Psalm 37:4) God wants to W.O.W. you with the desires of your heart, but notice the clause; first you need to delight in Him.

Delighting in the Lord means spending time with God every day, reading His Word, developing a relationship that goes beyond, "Help me Lord!" Delighting begins as a discipline that evolves into a love affair. At first you start because you feel like you *have to*, then you move into the realm of *want to*, and finally you get to the point where you *need to* spend time with God. God becomes your *gotta* have. He becomes more important than chocolate! I knew that would get your attention. Moms tend to be rather territorial when it comes to their chocolate. Why not develop the same kind of "don't mess with my..." relationship with God.

I know it's difficult to find time to spend with God when so many distractions pull from every given direction. But you begin by offering God what little you have and move on from there. He will meet you right where you are, with whatever you have, and love you regardless. Delight in Him and He will W.O.W. you in more ways than you ever dreamed possible.

⏰ TIME FOR HIM ⏰

Lord, thank You for all of the wows in my life. You are awesome and amazing! Lord, take me to the next level. Help me develop a relationship with You that grows deeper and stronger each day. W.O.W me Lord as I commit to delight in You every day.

⏰ TIME FOR MOM ⏰

Have you ever experienced a W.O.W moment; a time where God worked so profoundly in your life that the awe of it all literally brought you to your knees? Isn't it totally awesome! O.K. now I am sounding like my kids. But it's true. These golden awe inspiring moments stand out in our lives as points of reference. Kind of like when God parted the Red sea! Talk about a huge W.O.W. moment to remember! Or when Lazarus made his curtain call appearance! His life was over, the credits were running, yet with one W.O.W. word from Jesus an instant squeal hit the screens! Can you get any better than that!

Mom, I believe God wants to W.O.W. you in a big way. He wants to knock those pink slippers right off your feet. He not only wants to be a part of your life, He wants to *be* your life, your *gotta* have, your more important than chocolate! Let Him! (Dramatic pause) Let Him! (I know I am repeating myself, but when you're a Mom the propensity to repeat becomes habit.) Did you hear me Mom! Let Him! Delight yourself in the Lord. Make Him your main squeeze! (We are talking about a love relationship here. Remember!) Give Him all you've got and don't forget to put your name in for that next drawing. You never know. He just might choose to W.O.W *you* next!

⏰ TIME FOR TEACHING ⏰
Read: Matthew 6:33 and Mark 5:25-34
God wants to W.O.W. you! Let Him!

DAY 5

Overdone

*I tell you the truth, anyone who will not receive the kingdom of God
like a little child will never enter it.* Mark 10:15

"Judy, will you rub a little of this on my back? It's really been
bugging me lately." My husband asked with a thoughtful glance
my way.

"Sure." I complied.

My husband occasionally has back trouble. A little *Icy Hot* will
often do the trick to soothe his pain. I dabbed a bit on my hands
and began to rub it into his taunt muscles. Soon, I could feel the
heat begin to radiate itself. Dabbing a little more on my hands,
I rubbed harder so that its thermal action could penetrate even
deeper into his aching physique.

Suddenly he shot up quicker than a child released from a
time-out. He ran for the bathroom and darted into the shower
screaming something about too hot, too hot, as he went. I guess
the penetrating power of the ointment got a little too potent for
my poor husband. Shaking my head in frustration it dawned on
me that I had done it again. Overdone it, that is.

In that moment, I was reminded of the Valentine's party that
I had volunteered to decorate last year. I had so many neat ideas
on how to create the perfect romantic atmosphere. Why not incorporate them all? Well, I did. What should have been elegant
came off as gaudy. Once again, I overdid it.

Overdoing seems to be a reoccurring theme in my life. My
motto: when you have a task that needs to be done, overdo and
have some fun! At least you would think it was fun because I do
it over and over and over again. It just occurred to me, I even
overdo overdone-ness. Wow! What a revelation!

Why stop at making only ten craft items for my home business when I know I can sell fifty. It's just as easy to bake four
dozen cookies as it is two. Why buy only one clearance t-shirt,

when at $1.00 a piece I could easily afford to purchase the entire rack. With these overdoing tendencies, I am often left with a closet full of last season's crafts, cookies to feed the five thousand, and enough t-shirts to clothe all of those poor children in Africa. If only I could slow down and simplify, life would be so much easier.

God is like that. With all the complications and excessiveness of our world, He simplifies. He only commands one thing from us. We read it in Matthew 22:37: "Love the Lord your God with all your heart and with all your soul and with all your mind." One thing, that's all he asks. If we do the one thing, everything else will fall into place. The simplicity of it is so refreshing, so comforting, and so not-exhausting. Why do I do so much when so little is really required?

We like to complicate God's one thing. We think we must have our act all together before we can kneel before Him. We think we have to make mega-bucks before we can tithe a little. We think we need to have an entire hour of quiet before we can begin to pray appropriately. We think we need to be better, do more, have it all before we can even approach His throne with the proper devotion. What we fail to realize is that God's throne is not a throne of intimidation. As high and mighty and powerful as God is and yes He is all of this plus so much more, His throne is one of grace. All He requires is the simple faith of a child. He wants us to emulate the same pure all-encompassing love and trust for Him that a child expresses towards his parents. This is the one thing God requires. It's kind of like the singular love a devoted wife feels towards her husband.

As my husband emerged from the bathroom towel drying his sandy locks, I beamed as I admired his handsome physique. With a twinkle in my eye and a new sense of concern I squeezed the potent putty onto my outstretched hand. "Come here babe! I'll fix you right up. Let me try again."

☺ TIME FOR HIM ☺
Lord, You are so awesome. I love You. Thank You for making it so simple. Loving You and putting You first is all You really require.

Give me the sense to know when enough is enough and the fortitude to stop at that.

⏰TIME FOR MOM ⏰

Today's society screams MORE, MORE! We value achievement and stuff—lots and lots of stuff. Advertising campaigns only encourage our overindulgences. They seduce with the ploy that life is not quite complete without their products—and we buy it. When is enough, enough?!

God's economy is so radically different from ours. More is not always better. In fact more often gets in the way of better. What we really seek is essentially so simple. God has carved out a place in each person's heart that can only be filled by Him. Why fill it with anything else?

The message of the Gospel is so basic that sometimes we think there's a catch. There is no catch. It is straight-forward and easy enough for a child to understand. John 3:16 says it all, "For God so loved the world that He gave His one and only Son that whoever believes in Him shall not perish but have eternal life." That's it! You don't need to overdo it with cookies, crafts, or t-shirts to feel content. God is enough. There's only one thing you can't overdo and that is expressing your affection to Him. So go ahead, overdo it. Overdo your love towards God and suddenly you'll find that in comparison nothing else really matters.

⏰ TIME FOR TEACHING ⏰

Read: Luke 18:18-30 and Proverbs 11:28

The rich ruler thought he had it all; still he lacked one thing. Don't let the excessiveness of our age get in your way. There is only one thing God really wants of you. Give it to Him.

Take Ten

*Very early in the morning, while it was still dark, Jesus got up, left
the house and went off to a solitary place, where he prayed.*
Mark 1:35

Take a deep breath and count to ten. 1, 2, 3, 4…. Sometimes it
works and sometimes it doesn't. What we really need is space and
the time to count to maybe a thousand…or higher. That is exactly
what take ten is all about. It is breathing space, time alone, distance from everyone and everything…appealing, isn't it? Take ten
literally means you remove yourself from the situation in order to
step back and gain a better perspective. Sometimes all Mom really
needs is a little personal space without anyone jumping on her lap
or vying for her attention, just space, lots of space!

But oh how difficult this can be when little ones bustle about
so demanding of our time and energy. Even when our children
get older it still seems as if everyone wants a piece of Mom and
there are only so many pieces to go around. Today, keep a piece
for yourself. Purposefully plan your little escape, just a short
jaunt. Remember, you still have things to do, people to care for,
and dinner needs to be ready at 6:00. But for a short time indulge
and take ten. This is one time-out; yes a literal time-out, which
you won't want to miss. Go ahead Mom, take ten!

TIME-OUT TIPS
Shut the door and hide! It may sound crazy but it works.
Make sure your kids are safe and occupied. Videos always work
well. Although as a rule, television should not be your standard
babysitter. But desperate times call for desperate measures. Find
a quiet room, closet, bathroom, or even the laundry room and
shut the door. Take a few minutes to just breathe before they
find you. Suck in the serenity of the moment. Don't forget to *just*
take ten. You can't escape forever. Eventually, you must go back
to your children!

Mommy day out! Arrange a babysitter and then take some time-out to go somewhere by yourself or with a friend. Shopping is always fun. Go to the library. Take a walk. Enjoy a good cup of coffee at an outdoor café. Take a break from the everyday.

Plan an overnight! Find a trusted friend or family member to watch your kids for a night and then plan an overnight date with your husband. Trust me, its O.K. to leave your children. They will survive without you. Go to a bed and breakfast or just fix a special candle light dinner and stay at home. Take time-out to cultivate romance in your relationship. You will be a better Mom for it.

Date your husband at home! Once again find a babysitter that will watch your kids away from home. Then plan an exciting evening with your hubby at home all alone. Yes, all alone! Prepare a multi-course dinner and enjoy each entree in a different room of the house. Eat your appetizer on the porch. Put a blanket down and lounge in the living room over dessert. (Yes, you can eat on the carpet.) Turn up *your* music, dance, play, and have fun. Do whatever you want. The kids are gone! (For an evening) Try it. You may never want to eat out again.

Catch a conference! This is a take ten that requires some planning. Find a female friend and plan a weekend getaway at a Mom's conference. Several organizations such as *MOPS* or *Hearts-at-Home* host conferences specifically geared to re-nourish Moms. Check out the following web-sites to find a conference near you and then GO! (www.MOPS.org, www.hearts-at-home.org, www.lisawhelchel.com Mom Time)

Fast! This time-out has an odd twist. Take ten or fast from something in your life that has become too important to you. This is something that you feel you can't live without. It could be many things: chocolate, coffee, soda, television... Anything that you feel like you must have to survive. We need to keep things in proper perspective. God should come first. He should be your gotta-have. Fasting refocuses your attitude. Try it!

Sometimes we really do need to just get away. Plan a take ten and refresh your spirit with some literal time-out.

DAY 1

The Power of a Smile

A cheerful look brings joy to the heart. ... Proverbs 15:30

My husband is on the local rural electric board of directors which necessitates attending several *power* conventions each year. The kids and I often tag along for fun. This week we were enjoying one of those little trips. Sadly, our mini vacation was coming to a quick close. Gary was attending his last set of meetings while we packed. Afterward, we would load up the car together, and Dad would take the kids for one final swim. At least that *was* the plan.

I flipped on the T.V. in an attempt to distract my young ones when the phone rang. Gary's voice hesitated as he shared our timing dilemma. Check-out time was earlier than anticipated. This meant I had to single-handedly pack, load, and then wait for him with four kids in the hotel lobby. What fun?! Somewhere in our short conversation my mood shifted from up-beat to overwrought. I hung up the phone with a thud and then turned the T.V. up a notch as I grumbled my way through my new designated duties. The mess that moments ago seemed doable now screamed too much.

I managed to round up my little tikes while packing and loading the car. We made it up the hill, in the heat of the day to the main building. Now we were sitting in the hotel lobby. At least I was sitting. The boys rotated between balancing acts of standing on their heads in the leather upholstered lounge chairs, to a quick chase around the fish tank, to entertaining the guests with a wild wrestling match on the carpet. My baby was beginning to fuss and so was I.

As I tried to wisp back my droopy doo, I was reminded that my downcast demeanor was a mere reflection of my down and out hairdo. The electrical outlet had shorted out while drying my hair. Needless to say my styling attempts did not achieve radiant results. *How ironic,* I thought, *to be at a "power" conference without electrical power!* Managing four rambunctious children was beginning to overload my attitude circuits. If my husband didn't show up soon, I was about ready to blow a fuse myself.

As I caught a glimpse of Dad's face approaching, I decided to make sure he could feel my pain. Yes, I wanted him to experience a little guilt for abandoning me, some sympathy would be nice. It didn't take much effort to put on a face that shouted distraught, worn-out, TAKE THESE KIDS! Is that really so bad?

Right as I was at the peak of my most pitiful performance, an elderly lady, who had witnessed my misery, perked with a bright smile, "My, what a lovely family you have."

Quickly hiding my eyes from embarrassment, I thought, *Lovely, I was anything but lovely at the moment and had she actually seen my children's outlandish lobby etiquette?* I had been appalled. Now, I sunk into my seat disgusted with myself.

Yet, her smile tickled my conscience. Where was my welcoming grin, when my husband so eagerly walked the plank to meet us? Instantly, Karol Ladd's book, *The Power of a Positive Mom* surfaced in my thoughts. She had devoted an entire chapter to the powerful influence of a smile.[2] She was right.

Although, I wanted to instantly redeem myself, I thought it best to just hold that thought. I had worked so hard to look harried, if I put on a sassy smile at this point, Gary might deduce I was taking on bi-polar tendencies.

Later, as Dad rescued the kids from Mom for that promised swim, I lounged at the pools edge and reflected on my much needed attitude adjustment. After a while, Gary cautiously approached and inquired if everything was O.K. Remembering that dear lady's smile, with my attitude now properly adjusted, I perked up the corners of my mouth and reassured that everything was just fine. I encouraged him to have fun, be Dad, and save the day.

As he dripped back into the pool, I pondered, *I wonder, with all the important meetings delving into the efficient management of electrical power, did any of the board members grasp the simple truth that the most effective way to improve business was to cultivate the power of a smile?* (A rather lengthy pondering.) A smile can change your life and increase productivity. There is something about the high-voltage, electrical charge of a pearly grin that can send a quick chill up the spine and lighten the load of the most trying situation, even thirty minutes of juggling four wired roughnecks in a hotel lobby. Yes, a smile is a powerful tool! Hopefully, when I hit my next power outage, I will flip the breaker with an electrical smile. Smiles that will not only recharge my batteries but will also send out a current that will positively jolt everyone else around me as well.

☉ TIME FOR HIM ☉

Dear Lord, thank You for reminding me that a smile not only brings joy to my heart, it also radiates a powerful charge to all those around me. I pray that I will set the powerful example of a simple smile for all to see.

☉ TIME FOR MOM ☉

Have you recently experienced a power outage? These are times when the weight of juggling children, the home, and outside obligations overloads your attitude circuits. Moms, if we were blatantly honest, we would have to admit that sometimes, our days are not quite as difficult as we let on. We want sympathy. We want Dad to fully comprehend the magnitude of the difficulty of our job. We often accomplish this feat by pitiful performances when he walks through the door.

I am reminded of the commercial in which a Mom prepares a quick and easy snack for her family. In order to look as if she has slaved in the kitchen all day, she dusts her face with flour, adjusts her clothes, and tousles her hair. Let's be real. We've all done this, haven't we?

Instead, what if we put on a powerful smile when Dad finally comes home to rescue? Wouldn't that set a warm pleasing tone to the atmosphere of your home? Challenge yourself. Today, no matter what kind of day you have had, greet your family with a perky smile. See what happens. You may be pleasantly surprised at the results. Smiles are contagious. Start an epidemic today.

⏲ TIME FOR TEACHING ⏲
Read: Proverbs 17:22, 1 Thessalonians 5:16, and Philippians 4:4
God wants you to be happy. But it is a choice. Today, choose wisely.

DAY 2

What Did She Write?

And we know that in all things God works for the good of those who love him, who have been called according to his purpose.

Romans 8:28

I was invited to a Mother's day tea hosted by my daughter's third grade class. It was beautiful. Flowers decorated the tables as the kids entertained us with poetry and song. The main event was a game. Each child had filled out a questionnaire that best described their Mothers. Exchanging sheets, we were to guess which Mom each represented as they were read out loud.

I listened with peaked interest, curious to discover my daughter's take on me, her Mother. The first question was, "What is your Mother's favorite color." That was easy. Blue was my obvious hue of choice and Michaela knew that. So, I paid close attention for a "blue" sheet.

Finally, they came to one that sounded a bit like me. It stated that I was pretty, a nice compliment. Watering flowers was a favorite weekend activity. Well, that was a stretch but still doable. Then out of the blue, they read a question that knocked my socks off. The question was, "What is one important thing your Mother has taught you?" Her answer was, "To love God." A lump began to swell in my throat as I struggled to keep my composure. The surprise of her response stimulated an assortment of questions. *Where did that come from? Did I really do that? Did I hear her answer correctly?* As touched as I was by my daughter's reply, I couldn't help but question its validity. You see, Michaela knows the real me.

On the outside, I think most people would consider me to be a pretty together Mom. In fact, I coordinate a Mom's group. In this leadership position, you would think that I would be a model Mother, easily managing my children, the house, and all the volunteer work that we Mother's do.

Michaela, however, has seen the other side of Mom, the not so together side, the side that few have seen that only comes out behind closed doors. You see, she was there when I threw the potty seat across the room out of sheer HOW DO I GET THIS CONCEPT THROUGH TO HER frustration. Don't worry, the potty seat was empty. That was the problem! She was there when I broke my favorite wooden spoon on a pot of chili because THESE KIDS ARE DRIVING ME CRAZY! She has seen my worst! How could she possible say that I taught her to love God when I had been such a poor example? It just didn't seem achievable.

But, I guess along with my worst maybe she has also caught a glimmer of my best. She was there when I asked for forgiveness because Mommies aren't perfect. She has caught me with my Bible open as I delved into the Word for some encouragement and help. She has peaked in my bedroom when I was kneeling beside my bed in prayer asking God for the strength to handle the challenges of raising all of these kids. I guess because of my worst she has caught me lean on God more which is what we should be at our best.

Still, I just didn't quite get it. Michaela has seen the real me. She has experienced my ugliness. How could she write that I taught her to love God? The thought was overwhelming.

I knew it was only by God's divine mercy that my child could learn to love God through me. Maybe there was hope. Maybe in all the wrong, there was something right.

Thank You, God, for using me with all of my flaws to still bless my daughter by somehow teaching her to turn her heart to You.

☺ TIME FOR HIM ☺
Thank You, God, for sticking with me, for Your unfathomable compassion, mercy, and grace. I praise You Lord that through all of the bad, You can still use me to do some good. Forgive me when I fail. Give me the strength to set an example that teaches my children to lean on and love You more each day.

⏱ TIME FOR MOM ⏱

Have you ever had the fear that you might have damaged your children...for life? Join the club! Unfortuantely, babies do not come with how-to guides for direction. We all blow it at one time or another. And yes some blow ups are bigger than others and some more frequent. From a Mom that has blown it over and over again, I am here to tell you don't despair, there is hope. How else can we learn if we haven't first messed up? We live in an imperfect world and, as much as we hate to admit it, Mommies aren't perfect either. Our weaknesses can become our strengths if we lean on God and use them to teach our children how to overcome. How else can they learn to maintain self-control if they have never witnessed us struggle to regain it? How else can we teach humility if pride has never been shot down first? How else can we teach forgiveness if we have never had a need to be forgiven? We offer mercy and grace to our children because we too need it ourselves. 2 Corinthians 12:10 explains, "For when I am weak, then I am strong." It's the greatest oxymoron of faith. When we are weak, God is made strong. Your weaknesses become your strengths because in them your need and dependence on God is greater. Children see this and they learn.

I feel a need to interject a word of caution. I don't want to leave the impression that it is OK to behave badly. If crossing the line is a reoccurring theme in your home, you need to consider getting some real help. Julie Ann Barnhill's book, *She's Gonna Blow*, is a wonderful resource that addresses Mommy anger management.[3] Join a Mom's group such as *MOPS* (Mothers of Preschoolers). Find an accountability partner. If necessary, seek professional help. This is a one battle you need to win for the sake of your children.

Messing up is not something you want to intentionally do and if it is a serious problem you do need to get some help. But let's face it—real life happens. It's when we mess up and seek to do better that our children learn that although Mommy is not perfect, God is, and we need to depend on Him for forgiveness and the strength to be better. Use these opportunities to teach your children. Through your vulnerability God can work your mess for good. You too can teach your child to love God. But first, you need to love God and depend on Him yourself.

⏰ TIME FOR TEACHING ⏰
Read: Philippians 4:13 and 1 Peter 5: 8-11
God can use you even if you feel like you've blown it. Humble yourself before Him, seek His face and don't be surprised when your kids follow suit and do the same.

DAY 3

My Door is Always Open

The mystery that has been kept hidden for ages and generations, but is now disclosed to the saints… which is Christ in you, the hope of glory.
Colossians 1:26-27

Stepping into my bedroom I noticed that once again the closet door was left ajar. *What is going on? I just closed that door, didn't I?* I thought to myself. *Gary must be the culprit. He is always leaving things undone.* With a quick push I slammed the door shut while reminding myself to have a little chat with my husband later.

I thought the issue was a done deal until a few days later I stepped into my bedroom and there it was again. Only this time Gary was out of town on business. *Uh Oh! It couldn't be me, could it?* I questioned as my innocence unraveled before me. I tried to shrug it off but the lingering annoyance of it all sat on my shoulder whispering in my ear. The "door" was becoming an issue. I really don't want anyone happening in my bedroom and spying on my personals. Good heavens, what would they think?

Until one day, as I wandered into my bedroom to once again find my closet interiors exposed for the world to see, I hesitated. Allowing my frustration to fade, my practical side kicked in attempting to pinpoint the real underlying issue. *What was the big deal? Do I really have anything to hide? In a broader sense, is this the kind of person I really want to be? I don't want to cower behind a door. In fact, having the door open saves me a few seconds, which for a busy Mom is a real plus.*

I stepped inside to take a quick mental inventory of the contents of my closet. What was it that I didn't care for foreign eyes to see? I realized, to my astonishment, that it was just a closet with normal closet things. Would it really be so terrible for someone to sneak a peak? Do I really have anything to hide? Then I recalled all the times that I have concealed last minute clutter in my closet when company was coming, you know, those "works in progress" that haven't found a home of their own yet.

As I reflected even deeper, I realized that there were other things, intangible things that I often tried to hide as well. Bitterness, resentment, and jealousy are just a few. I guess I do have a few cobwebs in my spiritual closet. Unattractive "works in progress," that I don't really want to share with others, have a way of hiding in dark corners behind closed closet doors. My family has seen these things; but when the doorbell rings, they are quickly stashed away.

I am so thankful that I have a God that can straighten up the messiest closet. He can help me find a safe storage space for my "works in progress." Dark corners, dust mites, and cobwebs are His specialty.

The greatest mystery of all is that, when I open the door of my heart to Him, He will not only clean out the contents, but He will dwell inside me and continue to keep house. Above all else, that is what I want people to see. I pray they will catch a glimpse of Christ living within me.

So, if you happen to stop by, please, come on in and make yourself at home. If you do, by chance, wander into my bedroom; please feel free to look around. If the closet door is open, you might shut it for me. I'm not trying to hide anything. I just want to see if my husband will notice.

⏰ TIME FOR HIM ⏰

Dear Lord, You know the real me. You know my dark secrets and yet You still love and accept me just as I am. Help me clean house. Wipe away all my cobwebs and shine Your light through me. Thank You for dwelling inside me and help me to honor You by keeping my clutter under control.

⏰ TIME FOR MOM ⏰

What is in your closet? Do you stash unattractive "works in progress" when you know someone is coming over? When the phone rings, does crabby suddenly turn into chummy? Take a second to check out your inventory. Have you stored away bitterness, resentment, or jealousy towards someone in the dark corners of your heart? Maybe, it's time to do a little spring cleaning.

Did not know that God knows your deep dark secrets and He still loves and accepts you regardless. Open your door to Him. Ask God to clean out your closet and then invite Him to take residence inside your heart. When He has tidied up your storage space, you won't feel the need to run and hide the next time the door bell rings.

The rewards of an orderly closet are peace and contentment. What a joy to open a closet door (or in my case just walk in) and find all your personal belongings so neatly arranged, right at your fingertips when a need arises. You can feel the same satisfaction with your spiritual closet. God can realign all of your thoughts and attitudes to be in tune with Him. Ask Him to come in, do a little spring cleaning, and then rest in the satisfaction that you can leave your closet door open too.

🕐 TIME FOR TEACHING 🕐

Read: John 14:16-23 and 1 Corinthians 3:16

When you open your door to Him; He will dwell inside your heart. This, my sweet sisters, is the greatest miracle of all.

Rekindled Love

And I will do whatever you ask in my name, so that the Son may bring glory to the Father. You may ask me for anything in my name, and I will do it. John 14:13-14

William Riley has been the name on my lips lately, spoken not with endearing whispers, but with the bite of annoyed crispness. "William Riley, leave your brother alone! William Riley, stop that! William Riley, go to your room!"

Ever since we added a new baby to the family, it seems that my four-year-old son's behavior has become increasingly more and more intolerable. He just can't seem to leave his baby brother alone. He means well, but his continual hovering is extremely nerve-racking. I constantly find myself nagging, and yes, I have to admit, I really don't like this child right now! I know a *good* Mother is not supposed to have these feelings, but it's true. He is driving me Crazy with a capital C that rhymes with G that stands for guilt. Yes, guilt. Tons and tons of Mommy-guilt unloads on me for even entertaining the thought. Even still, the thought is there and I can't ignore it.

As I contemplated my disturbing ill-will towards my child, a faint memory floated before me. A year ago, before I became pregnant, Will, was my buddy. We were closer than bread and butter. He used to slip into bed with me around four or five in the morning and we would cuddle until the sun beckoned us up. I loved our predawn appointments. I remember a deep sense of love in his eyes when he looked up at me in those wee morning hours. The feeling was mutual. Back then tidal waves of affection flooded my heart. Will was *my* boy, my precious little boy. Nothing would ever change that, so I thought, until now.

Over time, my protruding belly pushed him out of bed and a new baby brother eventually took away his youngest status. Today, as hard as I tried, I just couldn't seem to muster up that longing, that fondness that seemed so natural back then. I couldn't get past Will's irritating behavior. I couldn't reignite the love I felt for this little boy just one year ago. As I sat feeding my new bundle of joy, I lamented my lack of desire for my son. *How could I be such an awful mother to actually question my love for my child? What is wrong with me? Surely, this is not normal.* The intensity of it all grew as I feared my thoughts might betray me and permanently hinder my child's emotional development.

Feeling a sense of despair, I took a moment to lift my troubled spirit up to God. *Lord, I have to be honest. You know my heart. You know how I am struggling to love Will right now. Please Lord, I beg of you, rekindle my love towards my son. I fear my constant badgering might somehow damage him. Forgive me for feeling this way. Help me feel the same passion for this child that I felt just one year ago.*

Later that morning, as I lay on the floor trying to exercise away my excess "baby" fat, Will snuck up from behind. Curling up next to me, he positioned himself so we could snuggle. We locked eyes and for a second, I thought I caught a glimmer of that same expression that I vaguely recalled. With a look of longing, his innocent eyes searched my soul as if he sensed my unease. Timidly, he prompted the question, "Mom, do you remember how we used to cuddle?" Instantaneously, that same rush of love, that joy that I thought I had forgotten exploded in my heart. Warmth wrapped itself around us as I pulled Will in, deepening our embrace. Caressing the softness of his little boy locks, I sweetly whispered my reply, "Oh William, *my* William, yes, I remember how we used to cuddle."

☺ TIME FOR HIM ☺

Thank You, Lord for answering the simple prayer of a worn-out Mom. You are a God that hears the sincere in heart and responds. Help me to always remember that You are but a breath away, ready and willing to help in my time of need.

⏰ TIME FOR MOM ⏰

Do you find yourself at times questioning whether or not you really love your child? Trust me, you are not alone. I believe it is perfectly normal to experience these feelings occasionally. At the same time, however, I feel that a Mother never really losses her love for her child. Instead, we simply momentarily disconnect from the joy that once came so easily.

The truth is kids can drive you wacky. They are needy, they fight, they whine and it is non-stop, relentless, a 24/7 kind of thing that grates on your nerves until there is absolutely nothing left of your sanity. (O.K., I'll stop. It's been a rough week.) Regardless it's true, children by nature can be extremely aggravating. They physically, mentally, and emotionally drain you, purposely pushing your buttons just because they can. At some point, we all lose the joy and yes, question our love.

One day as I was Mothering in the trenches, I finally, out of sheer exasperation, admitted to my youngest, "You are driving me crazy!!!"

His reply, "Mom, you are driving me crazy too!"

At least we were on the same page.

Ladies, trust me, you do still love your child. You may not like him, or her, or all of them. But you do in fact still love them. Like and love, though often confused, are actually two separate emotions. You can dislike someone's behavior but still have a deep rooted love that will always be there.

If you are living in the trenches right now, take a moment to pray. Vent your frustration to God. He can handle it. Ask Him to restore the love that you know is still there just underneath the surface. God will hear your prayer and often He will answer in the most amazing way. But first, you need to ask. Go ahead Mom, get to praying right now!

⏰ TIME FOR TEACHING ⏰

Read: John 16:23-24, 1 John 3:21-22, and 1 Thessalonians 5:24

God wants to answer your prayers but first you must go to Him.

DAY 5

Wrong for All the Right Reasons

All a man's ways seem innocent to him, but motives are weighed by the Lord. Proverbs 16:2

"Mom, my stomach hurts," spoke a voice that sliced through the silence of the late night hour. Startled yet groggy, I shook myself wider awake. Gradually my vision adjusted to the dimness of the room as I attempted to discern just who it was standing next to my bed.

"Will, what's wrong?" I questioned finally recognizing my son. Noticing his pained expression, my concern deepened. This didn't have the feel of your typical late night rendezvous with a restless five-year-old. Before he could even respond my mental inventory pulled out a file from the day before when I had taken note of a similar expression on Will's face. At the time he brushed it off; now in the wee morning hour I questioned whether or not he was really being truthful about his pain.

Then another file popped open in my mind of a like situation I had also taken mental notes on earlier that week. A friend shared her saga of a late night emergency room trip because her son's appendix had ruptured. As I sat there in the darkness of the night, the connection between Will's pain and my friend's story seemed more than coincidental. *What if Will's appendix was about to rupture as well?*

Pulling out the manual for child care and development, I quickly looked up the symptoms for appendicitis. Reading the illness's description seemed to confirm my suspicions. As I made my case to my husband, we both agreed. Better to ere on the side of caution even if it meant a late night trip to the emergency room. With a figurative flip of the coin, we decided that my husband should take Will and I stay home with the rest of the kids. No use in dragging everyone out in the middle of the night. So off they went as I lay in bed and began to pray.

As my pleas for my son made their way up to heaven, unease settled around my heart. The fervency just wasn't there. Yes, I was praying for my son, but for some reason my prayers were half-hearted as if I really didn't want God to answer. This was very strange. Of course I wanted my son to be well, didn't I?

As my mixed emotions unfolded, my twisted motives became apparent. Although I did want Will to be well, I also feared my diagnosis was incorrect. What if I had overreacted and sent my husband on a wild goose chase? What if Will just had a little tummy trouble and wasn't seriously sick? What about the expensive emergency room bill? As the tide rolled in the dark truth hit me in the face. In all honesty, there was a part of me that *did* want Will to be sick. Why? So I could be right.

The realization of it all made me sick. How terrible to want my child to be ill just so I could say, "See, I was right." As odd as it seemed, I had to ask God to forgive me for a deep hidden desire that wanted my son to actually be sick. Was saving face really more important than the health of my child? Obviously not!

After I settled my conflicting motives, I restlessly drifted in and out of sleep waiting for that telling phone call. Around 4:30 a.m. a rustling aroused me. They were home. I quickly discovered that my gut instinct had been wrong. As Gary explained the situation, I braced myself for his response. I knew if I had been sent out in the middle of the night on an unnecessary trip, I would NOT have been very pleased. I also knew I would want to *share* that displeasure.

Instead, Gary cuddled in bed next to me and with a gentle kiss, whispered "I love you" in my ear. Amazing! While my motives had somehow gotten all mixed up, Gary's never wavered. Even though he too had misjudged the situation, he was wrong for the right reasons. Saving face was not on his agenda.

God brought me to my knees once again. How could I have been so selfish to even momentarily wish my son to be sick, simply to justify my decision to take him to the hospital? I'm glad I was wrong and through God's great mercy, I am now wrong for the right reasons.

◷ TIME FOR HIM ◷

Dear Lord, You know my heart better than anyone else. Doing the right thing isn't always right in Your eyes, if my motives are misleading. Matters of the heart are tricky issues; things that I don't always fully understand myself. Help me to keep my heart forever true by keeping my focus centered on You.

◷ TIME FOR MOM ◷

Have you ever found yourself doing something that looked good on the outside, but deep inside you discover that your motives might not be as innocent as intended? Let's be honest. We've all done this haven't we? Like me, it may be a twisted desire for your child to be sick in order to justify your gut instincts and a trip to the doctor.

Hidden agendas come in all shapes and sizes. I could be as simple as offering a gift or service with a deep desire to be recognized for your generosity; or volunteering to help a friend with the expectation that they return the favor—SOON. Even when our actions seem well meaning and they are, we still need to reflect on whether or not our motives are pure.

When faced with these issues, give yourself a heart check. Be candid with God, confess your hidden agenda, and straighten things out. Remember, God knows all. It is better to be truthful, than to try to hide something that you really can't hide anyway. God can use these situations to teach us honesty and humility. Don't hide. Sincerely confess your ulterior motives even if it means being wrong but now for all the right reasons.

◷ TIME FOR TEACHING ◷

Read: Acts 5:1-10, 1 Chronicles 28:9, and Proverbs 14:2
God knows the hidden desires of our hearts. Read how one couple's selfish motives lead to their ultimate doom.

Pamper and Indulge: Just a little!

Give her the reward she has earned... Proverbs 31:31

Calgone take me away!!! We've seen the advertisement but do we really take the time to do it? Mothers tend to get so caught up in taking care of everyone else's needs that they forget to take care of their own. Pamper and indulge is just that. It is intentionally taking a few moments to take care of the caregiver. Sometimes all Mom really needs is a little treat, a little indulgence to lift her spirit and adjust her attitude back in the right direction. I've discovered that it doesn't have to cost a lot of money to pamper and indulge. The small things matter the most. Little extravagances here and there can do a lot to refresh one's outlook.

To begin, make a list of your favorite things: things to have and things to do. Little things that make you feel more feminine, more pampered, more ahhhh! I've listed a few below to get you started. But, feel free to add and delete to your liking. Once you've brainstormed your list, start to incorporate them into the everyday. Be careful. You may be tempted to *stay* in time-out with this one. Don't forget, Mom still needs to be Mom. But for a time, pamper and indulge. Go ahead Mom! Spoil yourself!

TIME-OUT TIPS

Take a bath! Put the kids to bed early and draw yourself a nice hot bubble bath with the works. Light scented candles. Put a portable jam box in the bathroom and enjoy soothing music. Read a good book. Add your favorite fragrance to Epson salt to make your own inexpensive bath salts. Soak your weary body and all your worries away. Then pamper yourself even more with luxurious body lotion and body spray. Top off your home spa with an invigorating facial scrub. Mix a little olive oil and sugar together for an easy homemade facial. Suddenly you've transformed from Mommy back to the woman you were B.K. (before kids.)

Splurge on good chocolate! But don't forget to have some M & M's on hand for the kids.

Tea time! Light some candles or cozy up to the fireplace and enjoy a hot cup of your favorite beverage. For me this is tea. You might enjoy cappuccino, spiced cider, or even a special blend of hot chocolate. I love to do this after the kids are in bed. It is a great way to unwind and just relax.

Read! Sit down and savor a good fiction novel, books that make you laugh and cry. Read for entertainment! What a *novel* idea!

Do the do! Have your hair done and enjoy a change in style.

Enjoy a manicure! Pamper yourself with a manicure!

Get cozy! This may sound silly, but one of my favorite indulgences is to cozy my feet with soft fuzzy slipper socks. They make my feet feel loved and Mom a whole lot more lovable.

Eat out! This is a wonderful treat for my family. We rarely eat out. Indulge and let someone else do the cooking for a change.

Give yourself a pay check! Moms in general do not receive a tangible paycheck for all the stuff we do. I say stuff; because a complete listing of a Mom's job profile could quite possibly fill a book and this is not that book. Have you ever considered paying yourself a few dollars for your labors? Be careful, if you are a spender this type of indulgence may be a green light for overspending. But, if you are a natural saver this could be a delightful time-out treat. Splurge on something small to perk up your spirits. Or save up and buy something big at the end of the year. My uncle stored his spare quarters in a jar and over a period of time saved up enough to buy his wife (my aunt) a diamond ring. (Hey, maybe I need to have a talk with my hubby.) Pay yourself! Try it!

This week take time-out to pamper and indulge…just a little. Keep it in perspective and enjoy the simple pleasures of Mom taking care of herself for a change.

DAY 1

So Much Potential

Create in me a pure heart, O God, and renew a steadfast spirit within me. Psalm 51:10

The freshness of my infant son breathed life into my fatigued soul as he contently nestled himself in my arms. Marveling at his newness, I couldn't help but ponder all the ripe potential bundled up inside his tiny form. At only five months old, he had already doubled in size and evolved into a curious, interactive individual. And this was only the beginning. With God's grace, he would continue to grow, change, and develop into the young man God has purposed for him to be.

Joseph's newness spurred a reflective glance. *I would give anything to feel so young, so fresh... so limber. (This child can eat his toes. I don't remember ever being able to do that.)* In stark contrast, when I look in the mirror I notice the beginnings of subtle creases around my mouth and eyes. Gray hairs seem to be popping up faster than I can pull them. My body hurts in places that I didn't even know could hurt. *I'm tired, I'm old, and I don't like it. I don't like it one bit!* I scowled much like a two-year-old with an attitude. *If only I could turn the clock back...* I fantasized. But just as a two-year-old rarely gets his way, neither will I. Time marches on. Moms get old. Such is life.

I am what they call a late bloomer. I was twenty-nine when I birthed my first child, thirty-eight when number four came along, and now as I edit my earlier writings, the number forty-something seems to fit. I say, forty-something, because there are days I actually need to do the math to figure out what that "something" is.

It's easy for me in this mid-life state to question, "What's the point?" When I look in the mirror, the collision of my past and future sparks the recurring uncertainty, *Am I making a difference?* Often, I get so caught up in the day to day chores of trying to cultivate order out of chaos; I fail to see the bigger picture. In the midst of raising toddlers, it seems as if they will never grow up and start to *do*... on their own, but the truth is, they will all too soon.

There is purpose in all the little things Mothers do. The bigger picture is creating a wholesome clean environment where our children can feel safe, loved, and be kids. The bigger picture is nurturing our children so they can grow and develop their own unique personalities. There is a bigger picture behind the madness of the moment. We just need to have eyes to see and an open heart to embrace it.

A second glance in the mirror reveals a different reflection. I see maturity rather than fatigue. Did you know that Webster's definition for maturity is, "being perfect, complete, or fully developed?"[4] (I guess they had the full figure Mom in mind for that last definition.) I believe maturity is age sprinkled with wisdom.

Over the years wisdom has taught me to seek God. When I go to Him, He will give me the fresh perspective, renewed vision, and energy I need to keep up with four little ones. In God's eyes, I too have potential. With that thought in mind, my stance straightens as peace and purpose wrap around the questions that now seem to be forgotten. (Memory loss, that's another sign of age which isn't always a bad thing.)

As Joseph (who is now four-years-old) dashes in from the other room and plops himself on my lap, my attention is abruptly drawn back to him. The laughter in his voice resonates in my heart crystallizing my purpose right before my eyes.

Though my days are numbered, they are not over yet. I have four kids to raise, a home and husband to care for, and dinner...I guess I need a plan for dinner tonight too. As I mentally put together my to-do list, suddenly the drudgery of it all fades into the bigger picture of its purpose. There is much to do, and with a new resolve I realize that I am just the Mom to do it!

� TIME FOR HIM �
Thank You, Lord, for each child so fresh and full of potential that You have entrusted into my care. Help me to see the same potential in myself that I so easily see in them. Renew my heart and invigorate my

spirit. Give me the vision to see past the mountains of laundry to the bigger picture and purpose in all that I do.

⏲ TIME FOR MOM ⏲

Are you worn out by the tiresome chores of keeping house and raising kids? Do you see your diet soda as half empty instead of half full? Take heart, there is a grander purpose that is often hard to see past the cookie crumbs on your kitchen floor.

Just the other day, as my daughter caught me struggling to carry just one more load of laundry up the stairs, she illuminated, "Mom, someday there will be an end to laundry."

"When?" I questioned with peaked interest.

"Someday you will die!" she teased. Now that's a positive attitude!

Although, we may not see the end to the many wearisome activities of mere existence, we can take heart that there is a greater purpose behind our efforts.

For today, look at your child's grubby face with fresh eyes. Instead of seeing all the potential mess he might and probably will accomplish that day. Think of all the promise that budding, young life holds. Look at yourself in the mirror and see past the age spots to the deep, inner beauty you have developed through years of sacrificially giving yourself to your family and others.

I have roses in my garden that seem to be in constant bloom. I love to cut a single rose and display it on my kitchen table. As I watch the rose slowly open to its full bloom over the course of the next few days, I am reminded that I too am like that rose. As I open myself up fulfilling my life's purpose, God's beauty radiates through me, touching the lives of those around me.

If the daily grind is getting you down, take a moment to pray. Ask God to illuminate to you once again the bigger picture. You still have potential even if you have a hard time seeing it yourself. Ask God to give you a fresh touch. And don't forget, someday there will be an end to laundry.

⏲ TIME FOR TEACHING ⏲

Read: Psalm 92:12-14, Psalm 138:8, and 2 Corinthians 5:5

There is purpose in all you do. Today see the bigger picture.

Whose Problem is it? Anyway

For we must all appear before the judgment seat of Christ, that each one may receive what is due him for the things done while in the body, whether good or bad. 2 Corinthians 5:10

As I walked past the bathroom, the illumination of an empty room caught my attention. Once *again* the light had been left on. *How many times have I told the kids to turn the light off when they leave a room? Evidently, I guess not enough?* I ranted while searching the room for the obvious culprit. *There he is!* I eyeballed my five-year-old son as he played unaware of the oncoming attack.

In that moment, a mental switch flipped that instantly replayed all the times I had told him, pleaded with him and yes, even yelled at him to turn the light off as he left a room. *When was this child ever going to get it?* I fumed.

Armed with my evil glare, I quickly caught his glance from across the room. With a voice that dripped with sarcasm, I exclaimed, "Looks like someone left the light on…again! Will, I know it was you. You seem to be the only one in this house that has a problem with this issue."

As he continued to play, oblivious to my mockery, the words that had just exited my mouth hung in the air as if searching for their recipient. Then as if a light bulb went on in my head, I realized that they were actually mine to own. Ouch! Will didn't seem to have a problem; he was happily occupied in his own little world of play. Flipping switches was the last thing on his mind. No, I was the one with the problem. I had the problem and that was the problem! Will should have the problem! But he could care less. *How do I get this child to care? How do I get him to "own" the problem? How do I get Will to finally stop leaving the light on!?* My mind raced at the harsh reality.

As I stood there stunned and a bit perplexed, I realized that in a stronger sense, the problem *really* was mine. How many times have I been too busy or lazy to figuratively "flip the switch?" My indiscretions were little things, barely noticeable or so I thought. But God knew. I too, needed to grasp that little things do matter. It matters when I keep the extra change that the sales clerk miscounted. It matters when I let my kids trash the waiting room at the doctor's office and don't clean up after them. It matters when I am too lazy to change the roll of toilet paper when I have used the last sheet. Little things really do matter. Like my son, I too needed to *own* the problem and do better.

Wow, all that illumination from a simple left on light bulb. Still a little shaken and humbled by the magnitude of my little revelation I stood there frozen as the truth of it all penetrated deeper.

In that moment, I mentally fell to my knees. *Forgive me Lord for all the lights I have left on, times I didn't take the time or didn't care to finish the job the right way. Help me to show the same grace and mercy to my own children that You so generously offer to me.*

Looking back at Will, I'd like to say that I instantly redeemed myself and asked him for forgiveness for being so nasty. But, Will had already moved on. I guess he had been nagged so many times that although he couldn't seem to turn a light out, he could tune me out. Looking up I mentally whispered once again, *Forgive me Lord. I see now that the problem really is mine. Thank you for a lesson learned in little things. I pray that now I can teach it to my son as well.*

☺ TIME FOR HIM ☺

Dear Lord, I see now that in Your eyes little things do matter. It's all about integrity, excellence, and taking that extra second to do the right thing. With little ones, the temptation to let things slide is often overwhelming. Forgive me when I mess up. Help me to be a better witness for You and remember that eyes are always watching.

☺ TIME FOR MOM ☺

Yes, we want our children to turn the lights out as they leave a room, put the milk back in the refrigerator, and pick up the candy wrapper that just fell from their hand. All of these little things are important. Let's look in the mirror for a second; do we always model these behaviors back to our children? Do you take the cart back at the grocery store or do you try to strategically position it and pray that it won't roll into another car? Do you pick up the trail of cheerios that fall from your toddler's hands as you merrily push his stroller through the mall? Do you lay that unwanted item that little hands flung into your shopping cart in the checkout line or do you retrace your steps and take it back to its rightful home?

I have to admit that I am guilty on all accounts. That doesn't validate my actions and it doesn't make it right. If we want our kids to get the message, we need to send it with more than our mouths. We need to model proper behavior ourselves. It's not easy. Little things take a lot of time and energy. But doing the right thing is what God calls us to do.

The funny thing is, the closer you walk with God, the pickier He gets. Soon enough God will not only convict you when your actions don't please Him, He starts messing with your thought life as well. Where once it was O.K. to think it but not do it, now He wants you to stop thinking it too. Ugh!

Oh, isn't it wonderful that God cares. He cares enough to discipline those He loves. God cares about little things and He cares about you.

Today, honor God with your actions and begin to teach your kids through your shining example.

☾ TIME FOR TEACHING ☾
Read: Ephesians 5:15-16, Psalms 119:59-60,
and 1 Thessalonians 2:11-12
Do what's right, even in the little things, not because you have to but because you want to please your heavenly Father. Your kids will notice and begin living up to the standard you set before them.

DAY 3

Three A.M. Strolls and Five A.M. Feedings

...for your Father knows what you need before you ask him.
Matthew 6:8

The brightness of the dawning day peaked through my bedroom window, beckoning me to wake up. Still groggy, an uneasy settling tapped me on the shoulder with the feeling that something wasn't quite right. Glancing at the clock, my suspicion was quickly confirmed. Pinching myself to make sure I wasn't still dreaming; my eyes twinkled with delight. It was too good to be true. Joseph, now six months old, had actually slept through the night not just once, but twice; count it, two nights in a row!

Just as I was about to settle in and really enjoy the quiet, a wave a panic jolted me. *Maybe something was wrong.* Silently slipping into Joseph's bedroom, I let out a heavy sigh of relief. Thankfully, he was still breathing. With a new skip, I trotted back to the warmth of my bed to relish the moment a bit longer. *If only he could make it one more night, this sleeping through the night thing just might become a pattern*, I thought with hopeful anticipation.

But no, the next night at three a.m. that familiar cry aroused me once again. Wrestling myself awake, I took a moment to just listen. *What does this child want?* I questioned as my mother mode kicked into high gear. The distinctive pitch of his cry signaled that this boy wasn't hungry; all he really wanted was for me to hold him. Allowing him to fuss a few minutes to see if he could settle himself back to sleep, I sighed, realizing that my luck had just run out. Taking in a deep breath, I begrudgingly kicked back the covers in an attempt to muster up enough energy to get up just one more time. Staggering to his crib, the notion hit me, *I guess three a.m. strolls and five a.m. feedings can't be checked off my list of Mothering duties just yet.*

As much as I dislike our late night rendezvous', I am often

amazed at how well I am able to interpret my son's cries. A Mother simply knows. We have our own communication system; a language of facial expression, body movements, coos, silent smiles, and a giggle or two when I am lucky. I know when he needs a diaper change. (Before the aroma has hit my nose) I can tell when he is just fussing because he is fighting sleep and when he needs to burp and just can't get it out. Even the times when nothing seems to calm him, and I think I have lost my touch, I lay him on the floor to cry for a few minutes only to pick him up and have him finally yield to my touch.

I like to think of myself as the master interpreter when it comes to my baby boy. We are together 24/7. I am the one that feeds, bathes, changes, cuddles, and calms him most of the time. I can read Joseph like a book, even better than his Daddy who comes in at a close second.

No matter how skilled I am with my interpreting abilities, I have a Daddy that knows me far better than I will ever know my son. He intuitively knows my thoughts, feelings, and cries. He knows what I need before I need it. He knows what I will do before I have taken action. He knows when my heart aches to the point that groans replace words.

Yes, sometimes he needs to lay me down to let me cry for a while, work myself into a tizzy, so that when the time is right I will yield myself to His touch. He is with me through the dark night, and He wakes me up with a gentle kiss of sunshine through my morning window. He is by my side as I take each baby step, feeding me with His Word. He, too, is with me 24/7, and He will never leave me with a baby-sitter.

Have you guessed yet? Who is this "Father of the Year?" My earthy Father knows me this well for a season. My heavenly Father is acutely aware of my every thought for an eternity.

Joseph's incessant crying abruptly brought me back from my wandering thoughts. Nestling my fussy son in my arms, I began the familiar sway to pacify him back to sleep. Looking up, I whispered a simple prayer for strength. God knows my need. He gave me this child, and I know He will supply the energy it takes to care for him. Strolling away the late night hour, I snuggled Joseph close as a familiar peace settled throughout the room. We both had yielded to the soothing touch of the master interpreter.

☉ TIME FOR HIM ☉

Thank You Lord for knowing me better that I even know myself. You alone understand my every thought, need, and desire. When I cry out in the middle of the night You are by my side, alert and prepared to minister to my soul. You are my perfect parent. Help me to always feel Your touch. Today, I rest in You.

☉ TIME FOR MOM ☉

As soon as we brought our son home from the hospital, people started asking the question. You know, it's the question that seems to be on everyone's lips, "Is he sleeping through the night yet?" I hate that question. Don't you? It always makes me feel as if it is somehow my fault that this child of mine can't make it through more than three hours without a meal. Don't people grasp the simple truth that newborns are not supposed to sleep through the night? Well intentioned friends don't mean to offend. In fact, just the other day I too caught myself asking my sister, who also has a newborn baby, the same question. Oops!

Don't worry Mom, even if your child is not sleeping through the night, because you can interpret and soothe your baby's cries like no other. You are an expert and believe it or not, sleepless nights too shall come to pass.

Just think, God knows you even better than you know your children. He knows your need before you have even expressed it, and He will give you the strength to get up in the night each one more time that is required of you.

Today find peace and comfort in the knowledge that you have a heavenly Father that keenly perceives your cries and is always right there by your side—even at three a.m. strolls and five a.m. feedings.

☉ TIME FOR TEACHING ☉
Read: Romans 8:26, Psalm 55:16-17, and Psalm 139:1-10
When you cry out to Him, He is there.

DAY 4

A Hug Back

Love the Lord your God with your heart and with your soul and with all your mind and with all your strength. Mark 12:30

He hugged me! I really think he hugged me! When I picked up my eight-month-old baby boy, he actually wrapped his little arms around my neck and squeezed ever so slightly. But I felt it and yes, I believe it was a hug. My thoughts danced as joy rushed through my veins electrifying the moment I had longed for. We've cuddled many times and I've bathed him in my own hugs and kisses, but this was the first time I felt that he had genuinely hugged me back. What a priceless treasure!

A new baby brings so many precious firsts: the first smile, the first giggle, and yes, the first hug. I do everything for my little one. My life literally revolves around his care. It's amazing that the reward of a simple hug somehow makes all the sleepless nights, stinky britches, and spit-up stained shirts (mine, not his) worthwhile.

As I savored the moment, hoping for a repeat performance, I was struck with a deeper question. God hugs me each day with so many little blessings of life. Do I hug back? Do I reach up to heaven and say, "Thanks God, today, I want to hug you back?"

God's heavenly hugs come in all shapes and sizes. Last week, God's hug came in a unique shape, and it was just my size. It was a once in a lifetime clearance sale on bras. They were only $1.00 a piece. Can you believe it? Ladies, this really happened; I am not *padding* the truth here. (Get it, *padding* the truth?) Never before have I happened upon a sale of *true double D* proportions. Anyway, I felt that God blessed me with a blowout bargain, because He knew I needed a *lift*. (Oops! I'll stop…promise!) My bras were literally in shreds. In fact, it was getting to the point that the many safety pins holding them together might actually set off a metal detector. God met my need and saved me a bundle. To me, my cart full of bargain bras was a heavenly hug.

There have been other times that God has hugged me unexpectedly. I never consider myself "lucky" when someone pulls out of that close parking spot just as I happen to drive by. Nor is it a coincidence when that surprising check comes in the mail just at the right time. As odd as it may seem, I believe these little perks are actually God's way of not only providing but also blessing me with His love at the same time. He completely cares for me just like I do for my baby boy. But, the question still remained, "Do I reciprocate—do I hug back?"

Later that morning as I contemplated the issue further, an odd quiet caught my attention. It was too quiet, the kind of quiet that sends a Mom into an Amber alert state of panic. *Where was Joseph?* More importantly, *what was he up to?*

A swift search, quickly disclosed his whereabouts and waywardness. Joseph had pulled the opened diaper bag off the table. Opening the small plastic container filled with baby formula, he was now having quite a little party with its contents. The precious powder was everywhere. Formula is expensive! What a waste!

In that brief moment, the answer to my question became clear. I was reminded of the woman that wasted an entire bottle of perfume worth a year's wage on the feet of Jesus. She poured out everything she had as a sweet, fragrant offering to God. It was as if God tapped me on the shoulder and said, "See, that's what I want from you Judy. Waste yourself at my feet. Hug me with total sacrifice, total surrender. Give me everything you've got."

The magnitude of the moment caught me off guard. So often I take God's care for granted. At times, I barely even recognize His presence working in my life. Instead, I need to sacrificially pour my love and service out to God with a heart of gratitude and praise.

As I picked up my son and began to clean up the mess, God hugged me once more through the simple giggle of my child. Moved again, I whispered a sincere prayer of thanks. *Thank you for hugging me each day in so many unique ways. Today Lord, I want to hug back.*

⏲ TIME FOR HIM ⏲

Thank You, Lord, for hugging me in so many different ways. You send a word of encouragement with the bright morning sun. In the afternoon, You whisper a gentle kiss with a warm breeze. At night, the comfort of a soft pillow and a safe place to sleep offers the security of Your arms. You provide and take care of me so completely. Thank You! Open my eyes to see how I can love and serve according to Your will. Today, I embrace You with my life.

⏲ TIME FOR MOM ⏲

Do you remember the thrill of your child's first hug? Or maybe you have yet to experience the sensation. The first smile, the first giggle, the first time your toddler utters, "Momma!" All of these breathtaking moments overwhelm us with joy. These are the simple rewards of Motherhood—our "hugs back" for all the many things we do for our kids. When we receive these simple gifts, our hearts overflow, prompting us to *hug* our children back, reciprocating the love.

God too, hugs you every day. It could be as silly as $1.00 bras and close parking spaces, as serious as the restored health of a sick child, or as simple as a hug from your little one that fills you with overwhelming pride and joy. Let your heart overflow back to God. Waste yourself at his feet. Live your life with open hands of surrender, open hearts of submission, and open arms that hug back.

⏲ TIME FOR TEACHING ⏲

Read: Mark 14:1-9, Romans 12:1, and 2 Chronicles 16:9

She broke a jar of the most expensive perfume, pouring it out as an offering to Jesus. Have you poured yourself out to Him? Go ahead; give God a hug back today!

DAY 5

Where's Willy?

*We all, like sheep, have gone astray, each of us has turned to his
own way; and the Lord has laid on him the iniquity of us all.*
Isaiah 53:6

There is one notion that city folks don't quite grasp... When
you live out in the country as I do, you don't just hop in the car
and run to the store for every little need that arises. It is one
trip to town with lots of stops that generally takes most of the
day. The thing is, because it takes so long, the option for Dad to
baby-sit is generally not a part of the equation. So the kids come
along. They go wherever I go, or at least they're supposed to.

Now you can imagine when you have a town to-do list as long
as your arm and four tired tagalongs in tow, that a trip to town
may not always be a merry making event. Today was one such
day. The trip was NOT going well. "Who can annoy who the
most" seemed to be the common theme chosen by all parties
involved. Needless to say, it wasn't much of a *party*. Finally, we
had made it to our final stop. Triumphantly checking off the last
few items from my list; I headed towards the finish line, relief in
sight. *If only I can balance my baby, an overloaded cart with a wheel
with a mind of its own, and three stragglers from produce to checkout,
I will be home free. Hurray!!!* I cheered myself on.

Finding the shortest line possible with the fewest temptations
for little fingers, I quickly maneuvered into place. Turning to
count and then recount heads, a bewildered three kept recurring.
Where is number four? Specifically, where is Will? I questioned.
Quizzing the older siblings, a wave of panic slowly crested as
the realization hit, my child was missing! *We were all together in
produce. How could I lose him in such a short distance?* My thoughts
raced attempting to retrace our steps.

Recalling Will's strange fascination with vegetables (He takes
after his farmer Daddy.), I reasoned that a cucumber probably
caught his eye and he felt obliged to stop and marvel. Letting
out a sigh of relief, I sent out my oldest, to stake out the produce

section to find our missing link.

As I watched my daughter search unsuccessfully from afar, an uneasy feeling settled within. *Where was Will?* With a 50/50 shrug (half annoyed, half alarmed), I contemplated, *Do I go help her and lose my prized place in line?* Instantly the response, *GO*, propelled me forward. A rush of adrenaline kicked in as we began the desperate search for our wandering Willy.

Soon panic took over. This child was not in produce. He wasn't hiding in the nearby candy aisle, nor was he roaming the checkout area. *Where was he? Where was Will?!* My heart, now pounding, threatened to burst out of my chest. I began to not just call but shout his name, completely oblivious to the judgmental nods nearby. As I hastily searched and screamed, the nagging question kept bobbing to the surface. *How could this child have disappeared in such a short time span?*

It was then that my answer appeared; the fleeting thought that I had entertained earlier that morning made its encore appearance. For a moment, only a moment mind you, the notion popped into my head that I really wouldn't mind losing Will in town, because he was driving me bananas! There it was, in black and white, the thought that seemed so harmless at the time, now a reality.

Had I actually wished this to happen? I confessed, ashamed that such thoughts could even take root in my mind. But they did, and now here we were. Will lost, Mom guilty of treason, shades of sin, and the repercussions that followed. Mortified, I begged God for forgiveness and the ability to find my son.

Maybe someone took him. The alarming possibility gripped me. Stunned and shaken, I began to urgently question one of the store employees. The clerk directed me to the service desk. Service desk!? He seemed to not fully comprehend the enormity of my situation. As I pressed the issue that SOMETHING needed to be done NOW, I turned and caught a glimpse of Will in the distance. Somehow he had managed to wander outside and was now making his way back into the store, searching for us.

Abandoning my cart I rushed to whisk up my son. A wave of emotion shook my body as the realness of what could have happened sunk in. We both sobbed in each others' arms. Pulling him back, I cradled his boyish face in my hands while stressing, "I almost lost you, William! Do you understand what that means?" His tearful nod confirmed that he did grasp the magnitude of his plight. His body stiffened as he geared up for a good talking to; instead I pulled him into my arms allowing the warmth of his body to soothe my racing emotions. Brushing his hair gently against my cheek I whispered, "I love you Will. Please don't ever scare Mommy like this again."

☻ TIME FOR HIM ☻

Dear Lord, I praise You that You are a God that seeks the lost. Like a wandering little boy, I often allow distractions to pull my focus away from You. Forgive me when I stray and thank You for leaving the flock to find me.

☻ TIME FOR MOM ☻

Have you ever lost a child in a public place? It is truly a terrifying experience. The sudden shock and panic of the situation triggers a deep instinctual lay-down-your-life kind of love that propels you to find your *baby* at all costs. The funny thing is, that just that morning, you sent the same child to his room with the hidden hopes that he might rot there because he intentionally scribbled all over your heirloom quilt with blue marker in an effort to creatively express himself! (I speak from experience.) No matter how our children infuriate us, we still love them completely and unconditionally.

God loves you with the same kind of passionate love, only even deeper. Have you let life distract you, or are you in open rebellion against God? Like my son, come back in the store and find your Father. Or better yet, stay connected with God everyday. He will lead you to the checkout counter. Don't stay lost. Instead be found! Come home and share in the celebration of your return.

☻ TIME FOR TEACHING ☻
Read: Matthew 18:10-14 and Luke 15:11-32
God wants to find you! Let Him!

Beauty and Order

He has made everything beautiful in its time... Ecclesiastes 3:11

Chaos! At this time in my life, while little feet still bustle about my home and smudgy hand prints litter my windows, chaos is often the best word to describe my surroundings. At times I raise my hands in defeat and allow myself to be sucked into the whirl-wind of kid created clutter around me. Then there are times that I dig in my heels and insist that there be some sense of beauty and order in my home, even if its lifespan is brief.

At first glance, beauty and order closely resemble work. Well, it is. But, the final outcome is a sense of accomplishment that far outweighs the effort put into it. It lifts your spirits which in essence is a time-out. Remember the definition: A time-out is anything that lifts your spirits and adjusts your attitude in a positive way. Adding beauty and order to your home are attitude adjusters. The end result perks your mood in a way that makes everything else seem more doable.

This past week I deep cleaned my pantry and five days later it is still clean. Shocking, I know! (No, I didn't lock the kids out!) Every time I walk in, I feel a shot of joy just to know that something in my home is clean and has stayed clean. (Are you with me ladies?) This week take some time-out to appreciate and add simple beauty and order to your environment. It will lift your spirit and give you a fresh outlook on the many demands of your day. Check it out—it really works!

TIME-OUT TIPS

Say goodbye to sweats! Get up, make up, and dress up. No, you don't have to do house work in high heels. Start your day out right by presenting Mommy in her best light. You will look and feel better. That's the point!

Say yes to flowers! Cut or purchase fresh flowers and display in a pretty vase on your kitchen table. A little splash of color can brighten any room and spirit.

Light the candles! There is something about the warmth of candles that softens the soul and takes the edge off of a trying day. Of course you must keep them out of reach of children. But, go ahead, light the candles. You will be glad you did.

Enjoy natural beauty! Step outside and appreciate the beauty of the great outdoors. Take a drive in the country or visit a local park and breathe in the freshness of your natural surroundings.

Music! Pop in your favorite CD and instantly the atmosphere of your home transforms. Music really does soothe the soul.

Organize a space! Take five minutes to organize or throw out five items from a cluttered area or drawer in your home. I know, this sounds like work. But, the end result is a wonderful sense of order and accomplishment.

Tackle a tough assignment! Set the timer and spend thirty minutes cleaning out that closet or room that you dread walking into. Over a period of time you will be able to pat yourself on the back for a job well done.

Organize your little labor union! Kids can clean too! If you haven't trained your children to help with daily cleaning, do so now. Post a job chart or assign daily age appropriate chores. Start small, don't expect perfection, and reward their efforts. Moms don't have to do it all. Teach your children to help out so you can have more time-out.

Create some Mom space! Set aside a small area of your home to be just Moms and decorate it with your own preferences in mind. Create your own little oasis and then train your kids to respect Mommy's space.

Beauty and order are little attitude adjusters that put us back into the right frame of mind to take on the toddler to teen world again. Take time-out to creatively add beauty and order to your life and then enjoy it before your kids discover what you've been up to.

DAY 1

Even the Flowers Find Time to Rest

Come to me, all you who are weary and burdened, and I will give you rest. Matthew 11:28

Finally, I found a moment to sit. *Exhausted* was not quite strong enough a term to describe how I felt at the moment. Cooking, dishes, laundry, picking up this and that were just a few of the many chores that had filled my day.

My seven-year-old son, Adam, on the other hand, had so much energy that I thought he would actually explode. It had been raining, so the kids had been stuck in the house all day.

He sauntered into the living room and casually asked, "Mom, can I run around the room?" I was so impressed that he actually asked before he burst into his little trot, I complied, "Sure." Taking advantage of every inch of space, he ran around in circles going faster and faster. He'd fall every once in a while, only to get up and go again at full speed. If I hadn't been so interested to see how long this child could last, I would have told him to stop, because just watching was making me dizzy.

As I sat, awed at my son's performance, I reflected on all the circles I had run just that day. Geometrically speaking, circles by nature have no beginning and no end just like many of the tasks I tackle every day. Laundry, I don't recall it ever having a beginning, and I have yet to see it's end. Cooking and cleaning dishes fall into the same category. Although I am only down to wiping two bottoms at the moment, there was a time that I wiped four out of five in my household. *But*, bottom wiping (I couldn't resist) is but a small sampling of my many wiping talents. I wipe up spills, spit up, throw up, you name it. I have even been guilty of wiping up giggles when they got out of hand. Tears, hmm, I magically wipe away tears to make boo boos better. Trying to keep up, often feels like a juggling act.

The next morning I was still wallowing in my little "circle" pity party when I happened to glance out my bedroom window at a flower garden my husband and I had carefully planted. As I gazed at the flowers, I noticed that through the night, the flowers had closed and just now, as the sun was beginning to break, their petals were peaking open once again. God, in all His wisdom, whispered in my ear, "Even the flowers find time to rest." I hesitated as the words echoed in my mind. The only things flowers do all day are look pretty and grow a bit. I accomplish a lot more than that. If they could find time to take a break and rest their weary petals, why couldn't I?

Suddenly, in one of those "Aha!" moments, I got it. In the morning, the sunflowers' pretty petals awaken to the bright morning sun in the east. Throughout the day, they radiate in beauty as they reach and turn towards the sun. As evening falls and the flowers face the west, their petals finally close for a much-needed rest. If only I could direct my focus on the SON all day, then, like these faithful flowers, I too, would radiate throughout the day and peacefully rest at night!

The intensity of that epiphany caught me off guard. I spend so much time running my circles all day long that I barely take time-out to seek God. I've always thought I was too busy to sit down and pray. Instead, I am too busy *not* to schedule moments with Him. When I seek God first, He will give me the time and energy to run my race.

Today Lord, I will keep my eyes on You. Although my circles of Mothering duties do go on forever, when the day is done, I can find rest in You. You are there with me, providing the strength for the moment and the sweet slumber at the finish line, because even the flowers find time to rest. Today, I am Your "Son" flower![5]

☻ TIME FOR HIM ☻

Lord, I want to be Your "Son" flower and keep my face turned towards You throughout the day. Lighten my step. Refresh my soul. I pray for rest, sweet rest that only comes from You.

⏰ TIME FOR MOM ⏰

What race track are you running today? The constant, repetitive duties of Mothering are enough to wear any woman out. If only we could get our eyes off the Kool-Aid stained carpet to look up. That's the answer.

As my newborn baby rests in my arms, his tiny porcelain hand wraps itself around my single finger. Although his hand is so small, so fragile, so perfectly delicate, his grip is anything but. He tightly clings to my outstretched finger as if by holding on, he has a sense of peace and comfort to know that everything is O.K. in his little world. In this security, he can safely rest his weary head.

Today, that tiny newborn has blossomed and burst into a full throttle turbo toddler. No more nappies are the recent trend. My race has just gotten a bit longer. No matter how fatigued and fed up I feel, if I can just keep my focus in the right place, I know God will give me the strength to handle just about anything. I need to wrap my fingers around my heavenly Father's powerful hand and ask Him to join me on this journey. He will give me the energy to make it through and provide the rest that I need at the end of the day.

What about you? Are you worn out, tired of running in circles? Learn a lesson from the sunflower. Today, as your petals open to start the day, fix them on the Son. Keep your focus there throughout the day until evening falls, everyone is tucked in, and you can finally lie down and rest your weary head. Be a "Son" flower! If God cares enough to help flowers grow, look pretty and rest at night, how much more will He do for you. Turn towards Him and be a "Son" flower today.

⏰ TIME FOR TEACHING ⏰

Read: Isaiah 40:28-31, Psalm 62:1, and Exodus 33:14

Keep your focus on the Son and He will give you the sweet rest you desperately need.

DAY 2

My Favorite Words

If you love me, you will obey what I command. John 14:15

"Mom, can you give me my spelling words?" Adam approached as I washed the dinner dishes.

"Sure, but I'd like you to take a shower and get ready for bed first so I can finish up and then I'd be glad to give you a quiz," I responded.

Adam looked up and for a moment I was overcome with the inclination to tease. "Come on. Come on," I pleaded as our eyes locked and I leaned forward with a silly swoosh of my head for emphasis, "Tell me my favorite words, pleeeeeaaaase!"

A shy grin beamed from his face. He knew exactly what I wanted. He knew the words I was chomping at the bit to hear. Shifting his eyes downward in an attempt to hide his expression, he intentionally mumbled, "O.K. Mom."

Ruffling his sandy brown brow I teased again, "A little louder please."

"O.K. MOM!" he exclaimed with a brighter smile and off he went.

For a minute I just stood there basking in the glow. Aaahhh! How I love to hear my favorite words. Actually, *O.K. Mom* is just one example. *Yes! Whatever you say! Sure thing!* Whatever the spelling, the underlying meaning is always the same. Each expression sings the sweetness of a Mother's most favorite word: *obey.*

It hasn't always been smooth sailing with Adam. During the tumultuous two's the battle lines were drawn and indented into the orange shag carpet of our former home. (It was a rental O.K.) A lot of blood, sweat, and tears went into the training of our troublesome toddler. At the time it seemed like an eternity. Today, I finally am able to reap the rewards of all those years of sowing. Today, he responds, "O.K. Mom!" Battle won! Mission accomplished! Victory! Oh, how sweet the sound!

You would think that a Mother's favorite words would be, "I love you Mom." Well, they do come in at a close second. But, if we were all really honest, I think most of us would agree (especially Mothers of the strong-willed variety of children) that the elation of the phrase *O.K. Mom* is equal to that of a standing ovation for the Mormon Tabernacle Choir's rendition of the *Hallelujah Chorus*. *O.K.* means I give in, the conflicts over, truce. In the end *O.K. Mom* spells obedience which in turn spells love. John 14:15 reads, "If you love me, you will obey what I command." Simply put, to obey is to love.

With Adam a battle has been won. He finally relinquished his will to our parental leading. When he is a teen, I'm sure some regression will require intensive retraining. We'll cross that bridge when we get there. But for today, *O.K. Mom* sure is sweet. Today, I savor the expression. Today, I whisper back, "I love you too."

☺ TIME FOR HIM ☺

Dear Lord, thank You for a child that obeys. As a parent, an obedient child is the wonderful pat on the back that says somewhere along the way I have done something right. Lord, help me to be that same obedient child for You. Give me a heart of obedience that not only pleases You, but also sets a worthy example for my children to follow.

☺ TIME FOR MOM ☺

Obey! Obey! Obey! How many times has this single word escaped my lips in exasperation as I desperately redirect my wayward child? Some of my favorite Bible verses to quote to my children are found in Ephesians 6:1-3. They read, "Children, obey your parents in the Lord, for this is right. Honor your father and mother—which is the first commandment with a promise—that it may go well with you and that you may enjoy long life on the earth." I like to stress the "obey" and "long life" parts of these verses. If you obey you will live many years. If not, well, you can read between the lines.

When your child is obedient, a healthy sense of pride swells up inside that confirms that something you've done along the way was right on target—it worked. Halleluiah! As trying as it is to raise children in today's world, these moments are golden.

But, let's look into that Mommy mirror for a minute.

Mirror, Mirror on the wall... Who's the most obedient of them all?

Hmm... And the mirror's reply is...

How obedient are you when it comes to traveling down the road of straight and narrow? What does that verse say again? "If you love me, you will..."

"I love you Lord. I really do but..." we plead with God after we've disobeyed once again.

And God's response is: "Blah, blah, blah. I've heard it all before."

No, no, no, that's not God's response. I believe that's *my* response. No, God responds with loving correction. Remember, He understands our weaknesses. He relates to our humanness. Christ's dirty sandals trod the same dusty road with the same temptations we face each and every day. Only He obeyed.

Moms, today raise your hands and surrender. When you're tempted to gossip—zip the lip. When you're tempted to snap back—tone it down. When you're tempted to overindulge—walk away from the table. Say *O.K. God*, let my will be Yours. Relinquish yourself to His authority and obey. Obey is a four letter word. But I believe its meaning could best be spelled, L-O-V-E. "If you love me, you will obey..." Today, love God with a heart of obedience.

TIME FOR TEACHING

Read: 1 Samuel 15:22-23, Joshua 24:24, and John 14:23-24

God loves his obedient children. Stop rebelling, give in, and WIN!

The Art of Saying NO!

Ask and it will be given to you; seek and you will find; knock and the door will be opened to you. For everyone who asks receives; he who seeks finds; and to him who knocks, the door will be opened.
Matthew 7:7-8

"No, Joseph! You can't stand on the table! No, please leave that drawer closed. No, Joseph. I said No! Noooooooo! No, no, no no nonono!" (Sound familiar?)

A speaker at a recent conference I attended quoted a statistic concerning Mothers with toddlers. She explained that the reason Mothers of small children are so exhausted is because on average they encounter nineteen confrontations an hour with their children. As the rest of the audience gasped, I remained unimpressed. If I kept a tally of all the times I have scolded, rescued, and redirected my toddler's misguided curiosity, I'm sure my number would be much higher.

You see, while other children sit quietly during church, I find myself frantically chasing mine down the aisle. Toys are of no interest to a toddler in my home. Kitchen gadgets, telephones, or just about anything that is almost out of reach are much more engaging. Getting into places that ought not to be gotten into is the goal and he will use any means possible to achieve this feat. At the moment, I am desperately stuffing animal crackers into my toddler's mouth in an attempt to distract his attention so I can type. So far I have tallied seven, no make that eight, no, nine confrontations with him in a short ten minute time span. No wonder I'm exasperated.

No is no longer a one syllable word. It is not uncommon to hear a long stream of no's strung together with varying voice inflections in an attempt to get my point across. Saying no has literally become an art form. There's the quiet "no, no". (Don't go there.) The staccato No! No! No! (As I rip another stray pencil from my son's clutches.) Finally, there is the frantic NOOOOOOO! (As I race to rescue...AGAIN!)

If only I could demonstrate the many nuances of the word, *no*. But, I'm sure you can recall them from your own experiences. Joseph has heard the word so many times that although he still doesn't grasp its meaning, he can gesture it. He is ridiculously cute when he vigorously shakes his head no. Often he loses his balance and then plops on the floor full of giggles.

As I watched him showing off his new *no*, I too found myself mimicking his gesture. Smiles lead to belly laughs as we rolled on the floor together. In the midst of our fun, I caught myself. *Why is it so hard for me to say yes?* With Joseph I need to say no for his own safety. But more often than not, no has become instinct. I spit it out before I have even contemplated my child's request. No should have its place, but *yes* should at least be introduced into my vocabulary.

I am so glad that God has a better perspective on this *yes/no* issue than I do. He is a God that loves to say *yes*. *Seek* and you *will* find. *Knock* and the door *will* be opened. *Ask* and it *shall* be given. (Luke 11:9) Over and over God whispers *yes* to those He loves.

The world often sees Christianity as so confining, too many *no's*. If only we could grasp that the *no's* are for our own good and safety. In abiding by the *no's* we find liberation and the word, *yes*.

I guess for a season, *no* must continue to be a multi-syllable word in my home. At least until Joseph can grasp the meaning behind the gesture.

Lord until then, help me be a Mom that also says yes. Yes to fun, yes to adventure, and most of all yes to You!

⏰ TIME FOR HIM ⏰

Lord, I am so thankful that You do say yes. Forgive me for being so negative. Please give me discernment and a heart that says yes.

⏰ TIME FOR MOM ⏰

We know how often we experience confrontations with our little ones. I wonder if calculated how many times they hear the word *no* in a day's time. I'm afraid the statistic would be astounding. We bombard our children with *no's*. Do they ever hear a *yes?* As I sat contemplating this issue, my daughter excitedly brought to my attention her prized show and tell project which was a cocoon that she had found and proudly displayed in a water bottle. Over a period of time, the creature inside had finally broken free and was now flittering about its plastic domain. Only what was meant to be a beautiful butterfly was anything but. Instead of shimmering painted wings, they had grown crinkled and brown and now were barely able to function as wings at all. How sad. The plastic bottle that was intended to be its protection had become a prison and ultimately led to the little creature's doom.

If allowed, too many *no's* can have the same effect on our children. We can only protect and shield them so much. There needs to be some freedom, some independent decision making, some *yeses* for our kids to grow strong and vibrant and eventually be able to fly away on their own.

Creatively create safe play zones for your toddlers. Empty a lower kitchen cabinet of all glass items and allow your little ones to have fun with your plastic cookware. Kids need more than toys. They want to play with Mommy stuff—safe Mommy stuff. Let them.

For older children, pick and choose your battles carefully. Decide where you won't give and where more flexibility would be appropriate. Allow them to make some of their own decisions and then hold your tongue when you don't agree. Often the most effective lessons are not taught, they are gleaned from personal life mistakes. Let your children fail occasionally. Next time, hopefully they will know better.

Most importantly ask God for discernment. He will guide you. Say no when needed and yes more often.

☺ TIME FOR TEACHING ☺
Read: Mark 11:24-25 and 1 John 5:14-15
See, God loves to say YES! Ask Him. You may be surprised. Just when you think God will say no, He whispers yes in your ear. Oh, how sweet the sound.

DAY 4

Too Many Kids

Sons are a heritage from the Lord, children a reward from him...
Blessed is the man whose quiver is full of them. Psalm 127:3, 5

I was assigned the task of organizing a farewell party. Having ordered the cake, I stopped by the grocery store to pick it up. At first glance, an obviously easy task. Add four rambunctious kids into the picture and suddenly *easy* took on a whole new meaning. Let me explain my dilemma. My toddler needed to ride in the cart. My son, Will, had recently broken his foot requiring him to ride along as well. The other two could walk but I'm not sure I could trust them to carry a cake. I've often considered myself a master juggler when it came to mothering but this task truly tested my talents. Determined to complete my mission, I boldly entered the building, kids in tow.

Amazingly, I managed to transport cake and kids to the checkout where a three for a dollar sign caught my eye on the candy bar rack. The sucker for a sweet sale that I am, I unwittingly gave the kids permission to each pick one out. It seemed like a good idea at the time. But I guess the combination of kids, candy bars, and a yes from Mom was more of a mix than I could handle.

Adam swayed back and forth studying the choices. Will insisted that he should be allowed to have them all. He *was* crippled wasn't he? Joseph began to grab whatever was in reach. Michaela was the only one that could make a quick decision. As I refereed the chaos, my focus scattered. I guarded the cake and helplessly attempted to corral my crowd forward. I was so distracted; I could barely write my check.

Noticing the confusion the baggage handler snipped, "You *had* to have four kids. You couldn't have stopped at three?" He really wasn't trying to be rude, but rude he was. Just as my mother hen feathers were beginning to ruffle, God gently brought to mind the many times similar words had crossed my lips. Whenever caught in an uncomfortable public situation where my kids were beginning to get out of hand, my flippant excuse was always, "Too many kids! I just have too many kids!"

I never thought much of the comment until now. The whirlwind around me suddenly slowed as the significance the statement insinuated became apparent. With a lump in my throat I pondered, "Which child would I give up?" If I have too many kids, the inference is that I need to give up at least one.

Glancing at my children as they fought over their candy selections, I considered each individually. Michaela, my oldest and only daughter, the apple of my eye, do I give her up? My heart skipped a beat. Well, what about Adam? Adam's soft, gentle nature tugs at my heart. Could I really give up Adam? William might be a likely candidate? My scruffy haired boy does try my patience. Yet, I believe life without Will would seem much too easy. That leaves Joseph. Just looking at my bleached blonde toddler jump starts my heart. He is my sunshine. Yet the question remained. Who? Who do I give up? Which child do I let go?

Each child's bent is unique and special. Each a gift and blessing from above. Like the many candy bars that graced my cart, though different, they all offer the same sweetness. With a new resolve I reconsidered, *Too many kids—I think not.* From now on those words need to be blotted out of my vocabulary. I don't have *too many kids.* I have just enough.

Yes, the cake and the kids did make it safely to the car. Too many of us had a sweet ride home—kids, chocolate, and a yes from Mom—a good combination. Who can resist!

☺ TIME FOR HIM ☺

Dear Lord, thank You for the gift of children. Next time I get frustrated, please remind me that my children are a direct blessing from You. Help me appreciate the diversity they offer and the joy they bring with an attitude that says just right.

☺ TIME FOR MOM ☺

You may be thinking, "I don't have too many children; I only have one or two." Or maybe you have six or seven and think four sounds like a synch. Whatever your perspective, any amount of kids is too many when their abundant energy and demanding nature compel you to feel frazzled. When the words *too many* make their way to the tip of your tongue, remember God placed each child in your care for a divine purpose. God doesn't make mistakes. He perfectly matched you with your children. Our kids, as challenging as they may be, are meant to draw out our best and work on our worst.

God reveres children. There is a special place in His heart for each child He creates. When the disciples tried to send away the children that flocked to Jesus, they were quickly rebuked, "Let the little children come to me." (Matthew 19:14) Jesus appreciated each child. We need to be more like Jesus. Yes, Moms do love their kids. We just don't always appreciate them, especially at the checkout counter.

Today, take time-out and look at each child with a heart of appreciation instead of burden. Pinpoint one or more unique personality traits in each child that you could not live without and write it down on an index card to keep in your purse. Next time you feel a little frustrated; pull it out to remind yourself why you love this child so much. Just think, God loves you warts and all too. Today, allow God's love to flow through you to your children and then celebrate and say yes to chocolate! Who can resist!

⏱ TIME FOR TEACHING ⏱
Read: Mark 10:13-16 and Psalm 113:9
Children are special in God's sight. Today see your kids through His eyes and count your blessings for each and every one of them.

DAY 5

A Thankful Heart

Be joyful always; pray continually; give thanks in all circumstances,
for this is God's will for you in Christ Jesus.
1 Thessalonians 5:16-17

At dinner the boys often squabble about who gets to pray over the meal. We try to be fair and let them take turns. Adam generally prays the "God is great, God is good, let us thank Him for our food...," a prayer that he learned in kindergarten. William, on the other hand, has his own unique style.

In his four-year-old fashion, it often goes something like this: "Thank you Lord for Mom and Dad. Thank you for Michaela and Adam. Thank you for the food and the ketchup. Thank you for the forks and the spoons and the knives. Thank you for the napkins and the salt and pepper. Oh, and thank you for Willy and Zach (his cousin and cohort in crime) because they are very special. Amen."

I can't help but giggle to myself and think, *Yes Willy, you are special. In your childlike innocence you give God thanks for all things, even the silverware on the table.*

Oh, to praise God and thank Him for all things. I am humbled by my William. How often do I take for granted the many gifts, big and small that God bestows on me each and every day? I am so blessed to have a beautiful home, a warm bed at night, food on my table, and a wonderful healthy family to share it all with. Yet, I still find myself grumbling. I still have a heart that says more instead of just enough.

Exhibiting a contented and thankful attitude is difficult in a world that screams more, more. Advertisements coercively convince us that enough is not enough. In order to be truly happy, we need this and this and this. It's a shame, because our society has been blessed with so much yet we never seem quite satisfied. Unfortunately, I see this same discontent desire for more reflected in my children as well.

Just the other night as I tucked Adam into bed, he confessed that he thought he was breaking one of the Ten Commandments. I knew exactly what he was talking about. He had recently received a new *Lego* magazine in the mail and now was drooling over the many tantalizing kits displayed. Even though his shelves were lined with *Lego* creations, it was just not enough. He simply wanted more.

It was refreshing to see my son recognize his own failing. He knew he should be thankful for what he had. Yet, the overwhelming urge to covet more was just a little too much. It's an easy trap to fall into.

Before we built our home, I too struggled with a heart of discontent. It seemed that everyone else owned their own home while we still rented. I tried to convince myself that it wasn't so bad. We did have a roof over our heads, even though it did leak. God brought me down a long road of submission before I could lay my request for a home at his feet with a proper attitude that was inline with Him.

Paul said it best in his letter to the church in Philippi, "…I have learned the secret of being content in any and every situation whether well feed or hungry, whether living in plenty or in want." (Philippians 4:12) I believe the secret he is referring to is a spirit of thankfulness. An attitude that says, "I trust You to provide Lord and I will be satisfied with whatever provision You send my way." A thankful heart, that's what God desires.

I believe I need to learn a lesson from my boy. I need to thank God for all things and in all circumstances of life. He is the great provider. Only He knows what is best for me. I need to thank God for all things…even the silverware on the table.

🕘 TIME FOR HIM 🕘

Thank You, Lord, for a lesson in gratitude. You bless me in so many ways, how do I number them? Give me a thankful heart: one that appreciates Your gifts and doesn't ache for more.

🕘 TIME FOR MOM 🕘

I believe that one of the major factors of depression in today's world is a lack of thankfulness. Instead of focusing on what we do have, our vision is distracted by what we don't have and want--really bad. The grass always seems greener on the other side of the fence. What we don't comprehend is that it takes more time to tend that greener field.

When we finally got our new home, I quickly discovered that we forgot to install that self-cleaning feature that all new homes should have. Yes, the grass was greener but it took more work to keep it that way.

There is always something: something more to want, something to be dissatisfied with, and something to complain about. There always will be. Instead, we need to shift our focus to what we have, what we enjoy, and simply praise God for it. A grateful heart is a happy heart. To find peace and joy in this world, we need to practice being thankful.

Take a few minutes to offer a prayer of thanks to God for all the little things of life. Thank Him for dishwashers, dryers, and disposable diapers (do you really want to go back to cloth ones); microwaves, midnight feedings, and make up (I can't go anywhere without make up); chocolate, Chinese food, and children's videos (Can you imagine life without videos?).

And please, don't forget to thank Him for the silverware. Praise God and experience the happiness that a grateful heart has to offer.

⏲ TIME FOR TEACHING ⏲
Read: Colossians 2:6-7, Colossians 4:2, and Psalm 28:7
Over and over the Bible calls us to be thankful. Count your blessings. Name them one by one. And then offer up a simple prayer of thanks.

Create

She selects wool and flax and works with eager hands.
Proverbs 31:13

Dinner—check, dishes—check, laundry—check, dream on…
check. We would love to check all of these tasks off our to-do
list, but the simple truth is, they will never be checked off, at least
not permanently. Well, I guess they will some day, remember (to
quote my daughter), "Someday you will die, Mom!" (Such up-
beat outlooks I instill in my children…hmm.)

The ongoing daily chores of mothering leave us with a forever
feeling of undone-ness. That is why create is such a fun time-out
activity. By create, I mean make something. Something that stays
done. Something you can check off a to-do list. Something that
you can say, "Honey, look what I did today!" and feel a sense of
achievement that your efforts resulted in something more than
clean clothes and dinner on the table. Not only do you feel a
wonderful sense of accomplishment but you have something to
show. Now that's exciting!

I love to create. In fact I can easily get lost in creating. So, keep
it in perspective, but try it. You too may find that this is one of
your favorite time-out activities.

TIME-OUT TIPS

Craft! For those of you gifted with the craft gene let those
creative juices flow by pulling your resources and talents together
to make something that adds beauty to your home or can be used
as the perfect gift for someone special.

Scrapbook! Scrapbooking is a wonderful creative activity. It
allows you to artistically store those family memories and me-
mentos in an attractive story book style that will be treasured for
years to come.

Cook! For those of you that are genetically impaired when it comes to crafting, maybe cooking is your art form. I have a sister whose creative canvas is her kitchen. She soufflés circles around me. Another sister has mastered the art of cake decorating. Her scrumptious creations make any celebration truly memorable.

Sew! If sewing an article of clothing is too much, try your hand at Appliqué. It is an easy alternative that takes a fraction of the time with satisfying results. Purchase a ready made T-shirt, sweatshirt, or tote. Iron your fabric scraps to a fusible fabric bonder such as *Heat-N-Bond lite.* Trace and cut out your design. Then iron it on your chosen item. Finally, sew around the edges with a loose satin or zigzag stitch. It takes practice but it is fun and quick way to enjoy sewing that doesn't require as much skill.

Garden! Maybe you have a hidden green thumb that is just budding to blossom. Go ahead, dig some dirt, and cultivate a flower or vegetable garden.

Teach! I have another sister that creatively expresses herself through teaching. She volunteers once a week at her child's preschool. She enjoys creating fun activities to teach the children German. (Yes, I have a lot of sisters!)

My point is the possibilities are endless. You don't have to be crafty to create. Find your niche and then allow yourself some Mommy time-out to make something—anything that is your own. You just might surprise yourself. When I let my creative juices flow a home-based sewing and craft business was born. My creative energies now bring home a little bacon. Who knows, maybe God has a home-based business in mind for you too. Or maybe you can just enjoy the simple pleasure of creating something of your own that doesn't involve play dough or finger paints. Take time-out to creatively express yourself and then enjoy the fruits of your labors.

DAY 1

A Musical Heritage

I will praise the Lord all my life. I will sing praise to my God as long as I live. Psalm 146:2

Glancing over at my husband, we exchanged sentimental smiles as a warm glow filled our van. The baby had started fussing and Michaela, our oldest, naturally started to soothe him with a simple melody. Soon the other kids joined in and the whole van harmoniously swayed as they all instinctively sang together to calm their little baby brother. As I sat there taking it all in, I couldn't help but remember how Grandma used to sing to me in much the same way when I was a child. Her love for music has been passed down through the years and was now being passed along to yet another generation.

There is a musical heritage in the sap that spurs on the growth of my family tree. Its rhythmic beat pulsates as it is passed down from one generation to the next. I can still feel the warmth of Grandma's lap and the sweet sounds that vibrated from her lips as we rocked away many a long afternoon to the melodies of her favorite church hymns from the past.

She passed on her love of music to my Mother, an accomplished church organist and choir director. Many a Sunday my sisters and I quietly tip toed up to the balcony in an attempt to sneak up from behind and startle her enough to interrupt her musical postlude. We never succeeded. Mom was good! As much as we tried, nothing could sway her focus. She always has and still does pour her heart out into her music. She carefully chooses each musical selection to specifically enhance the message given at each church service. She has a burning passion for music. That fire continues to blaze in me.

Clarinet was my instrument of choice in High School. I remember driving my family crazy with long winded recitals in the kitchen and bathroom of all places. (The acoustics always seemed a little bit better there.) I majored in music in college and even went on later to achieve a master's degree in music education. My love went beyond concerts in the bathroom to a career of teaching.

Now, that pulsating musical life blood is passed on from me to my children. When my children were babies, they each had their own Mommy invented song that I sang to calm their fussiness. These simple melodies weren't profound by any means but it was their personalized melody and theirs alone. I see now that my kids, now older, are in turn passing on the same tradition to their baby brother.

Music is a wonderful gift God has given us. In my home hangs a framed saying that reads, "Bach gave use God's Word. Mozart gave us God's laughter. Beethoven gave us God's fire. God gave us music that we might pray without words." (Author unknown) How profound. Isn't that what music should be, can be, ought to be, prayer without words. It is allowing the soul to reach up to heaven in song as a form of praise and prayer with a bonded heart bursting with joy. It is getting in tune with God in the everydayness of a kitchen by singing along to the music on a local Christian radio station. It is simple acts of worship, like driving along with a van full of kids as they sing *Jesus loves me* to soothe their baby brother. That's the tradition I would like to pass on to my children. Not only to love music but to use it to praise God, to pray without words. God gave us the gift, it is our job to use it for His glory and pass it on.

⏰ TIME FOR HIM ⏰

Thank You, Lord for the gift of music. My voice may crack and my melody may be a bit out of tune but if I sing my praise to You with a sincere heart, I believe You can dub out my musical flaws. Help me to pass on my love for music to my children. Give them a discerning heart to distinguish what kind of music glorifies You. Thank You for the gift. I pray I will always use it to praise You.

⏲ TIME FOR MOM ⏲

Mothers naturally sing to their children. Lullabies and silly songs often flow from our lips. Is music that praises God a part of your daily repertoire? I enjoy listening to my local Christian radio station. When the kids were little, I cradled them up in my arms while dancing, twirling, and dipping (they always loved the dip) around the kitchen to the latest Christian pop rock music. What kind of music are you listening to and what are you passing along to your children?

There is an abundance of music on the market these days. We are literally bombarded with listening choices. Not all of which are very edifying. The melodic line is a matter of taste and does not determine value. Lyrics, on the other hand, speak volumes in more ways than one. When children are younger much of what they hear is determined by you. What station is your radio tuned in to?

I've discovered that there are Christian alternatives to just about every style of music out there: rap, rock, easy listening, you name it. Why not chose music that glorifies God? Children learn by our examples. I've found that my kids tend to like what I like—at least initially. Pass on a musical heritage that pleases God. Choose to listen to music with a Christian focus.

Often, the times I feel the most in touch with God are when I am singing these songs from my heart, with my mind focused on Him. Try it. Find a Christian radio station or purchase a praise CD from a local Christian book store. Sing along, lift up your hands, and praise God with your voice. It's one's attitude not the quality of the singing that counts. You might find your kids joining you in your little jam sessions. Choose music that edifies God and pass on a musical heritage worthy in his sight.

⏲ TIME FOR TEACHING ⏲

Read: Isaiah 12:5-6, Psalm 47, and Ephesians 5:19

What kind of music are your children gleaning from your example? Choose music that pleases God and leave behind a heritage that is worthy of passing on.

Two Sides of a Coin

Blessed is the man who perseveres under trial, because when he has stood the test, he will receive the crown of life that God has promised to those who love Him. James 1:12

My toddler restlessly rolled between me and my husband. *I wish he would settle down.* I thought to myself a bit agitated. As I lay beside him hopelessly attempting to pat him back to sleep, I couldn't help but reflect on how we ended up, soaked to the bone, in this shall I say "no star" hotel. Yesterday was to be the beginning of our family camping vacation. But, somehow we ended up here in a fleabag hotel instead.

That morning, packed and ready to go, we headed out for our first destination. The campground was beautiful. Picking out a wooded site, we parked as Dad began the process of setting up. Sensing something was amiss, he proceeded with caution as he cranked up the top of our pop-up camper. With each turn of the crank the tension in the cable increased until suddenly it snapped like a dry twig. The enormous weight of the air conditioning unit on top of the roof forced the back end to collapse with a loud crash. The front, to our astonishment, remained upright. We both stood there in a daze, shocked and sickened by the sudden turn of events. A hush swept over the entire family as we all stared at our twisted camper top much like a family of deer caught in on coming traffic.

"What are you going to do now?" I questioned, intentionally passing the buck to the head buck, you know, the daddy deer, my husband. This job was obviously out of my league, a job for a *real* man. *Let's see what kind of "real" man you are Gary?* I sarcastically thought to myself eager to observe how he intended to fix this problem.

Enlisting the help of some other *real* men from nearby campsites, they feverously worked together in an attempt to put the entire top down so we could at least pack up the camper to take home. It was then that the rain started. Actually, it was more like a downpour! Hustling the kids into the van, we watched from the sidelines as the men labored to no avail. Concluding that the situation was indeed hopeless, Gary's drenched recruits slowly abandoned him one by one.

As Gary, now filthy and soaked, got into the car to rethink the situation, I couldn't help but feel a deep sense of respect and awe for my sweet husband. Most men would have been kicking and cussing at that camper. Yet, my husband, a *real* man, remained cool and in-control. It was utterly amazing.

In that brief moment, I was struck with the image of a coin. Although a coin is a single object, it has two very different sides. Each day we face difficult trials, *coins* are thrown at us from all different directions. Through each life catastrophe, we have a choice. We must choose a side. We can allow the sticky situation to make us better or bitter. It is so tempting to throw in the towel, give up, and get angry. Gary could have easily thrown a fit—who could blame him. Instead, he chose to set an example of calm in the midst of chaos. What a blessing. What a profound lesson our kids gleaned from Dad on that dismal night.

As Gary went back out in the rain to face the situation again, a new stranger happened along. We never learned his name. All we know is that he was a Father looking for his son and for some odd reason (maybe divine intervention) couldn't find him just yet. He stayed with Gary in the downpour and helped him get the top down. Leaving the camper behind, we headed to town to find a safe dry haven for the night.

Sometimes it is difficult to see the shiny side of the coin in the murky waters of life's wishing well. When tempted to give in to despair, we need to flip the coin and concentrate on what is right instead of all that is wrong.

Taking in a second glance at my surroundings, I realized that our hotel accommodations weren't all that bad. It was an extra large room that was quiet and cheap. The mildewed shower curtain just made the place a bit more "homey."

As I finally calmed my baby boy back to sleep, I felt God's reassuring touch gently pat me as well. I struggle in life, just like my restless son. If only I could yield myself to my Father's comforting hand, He would grant me calm in the eye of the life's storms.

There are two sides to every coin. I pray that I can live by my husband's example and respond in a manner that is always pleasing to God.

☽ TIME FOR HIM ☽

Lord, why does life have to be so difficult. At times, it seems as if everything goes wrong. Through all of life's ups and downs, help me to hold fast to You. I pray that I would resist the temptation to behave poorly. Use these trials to make me stronger, wiser, and walk closer to You.

☽ TIME FOR MOM ☽

When trouble strikes, which side of the coin is your focus? Do you allow difficulty to get the best of you or do you take a deep breath, keep your cool, and grow stronger? God never promised that life would be easy. In fact 1 Peter 4:12-13 reads, "Dear friends, do not be surprised at the painful trial you are suffering, as though something strange were happening to you. But rejoice that you participate in the sufferings of Christ..."

Did you know that God is more interested in how you respond to trials than the trials themselves? Through the many storms of life, we shouldn't trust our feelings; instead, we need to keep our eyes on God. Life may be out of our control, but it is not out of His. God uses difficult situations to gradually shape us each day to be more like Him.

Next time life gets you down, simple don't let it. Don't give in to anger and despair. Instead, flip the coin and focus on the brighter side. There always is one. Ultimately, the heads or tails of each situation is up to you. Today, choose wisely.

☽ TIME FOR TEACHING ☽

Read: 1 Peter 1:6-9, Romans 5:3-5, and Acts 16:22-26
Jesus' followers suffered many trials as they sought to spread the Word. Instead of getting discouraged they rejoiced in their suffering. Don't be tempted to harbor bitterness and anger. Flip the coin and find joy and peace through Christ.

DAY 3

No Bones in My Belly

…O Lord, God of heaven, the great and awesome God, who keeps his covenant of love with those who love him and obey his commands,
Nehemiah 1:5

As I poured the milk for our evening meal, Will curiously pondered out loud, "Mom, why do we have to drink milk?" Michaela, who had recently become an expert on the subject through extensive study for a food's unit test at school, responded promptly and with great authority, "Milk is good for your bones, Will!" I could tell the wheels were turning in my three-year-old son's head as he thought through her answer. After a few moments of careful consideration, he briskly remarked, "But I don't have any bones in my belly!"

I had to laugh. Will just didn't *get it* and I was not about to try to expound on how the calcium enriched chemical qualities of milk actual do strengthen the bones—even if there aren't any bones in your belly. Because, to be honest, I'm not sure if I actually *get it* either. What we all did get, however, was a good giggle that night

Later that evening, as I reflected on our humorous moment, I was struck with a more serious thought. I, in my finite understanding *don't get* the awesomeness of God. I am but a mere speck on this vast planet, and yet God knows me by name. He has every hair on my head counted. That thought simply blows me away.

What's even more amazing is that He seeks to intimately have a relationship with me. "Why me?" is the question. I am the wacky Mom that uses the term "stinker butt" as a loving term of endearment for my kids. (Yes, I have to admit I did use this term in a funny affectionate sort of way, mind you.) I am that obsessive Mom that has to produce one hundred of every craft item I make in order to experience creative fulfillment. I am the Mom that never has learned to count past three, although my kids do. Often, they continue for me. (Four, five, six... Oh! I hate when they do that.) Why would God, in all His greatness, not only desire but pursue a companionship with a wacky, obsessive, controlling Mom like myself. It is one of the greatest mysteries that I, in my limited humanness, will never completely grasp.

Looking back to my mischievous little boy, my heart filled with hope and a prayer for him.

So, Will, even if you "don't get" how milk can be good for your bones when you don't have any bones in your belly, I hope that some day you will get that God loves you with a love greater than anything I have to offer. He knew you before you were born, as you were knit together in my womb. He longs to share an intimacy with you as you let go of boyish behaviors to mature and become a man.

I pray, one day, when the time is right, you will "get it" and ask Him to be Lord of your life. Even with all your wild Willy wanderings, He calls you by name. He alone provides nourishment for your soul that surpasses anything an enriched glass of milk can do for your bones. Say "Yes!" to Him Will, and "get" more than you ever dreamed possible.

⊙ TIME FOR HIM ⊙

Oh God, You are so awesome, so huge, and so perfect. With a mere utterance from Your lips You brought the expanse of the universe and all it holds into existence. You are the ultimate, the great I Am, the forever. I am awestruck that You would even bother to know me. Become real to me, reveal Yourself, so that I can get it and get to know You.

⊙ TIME FOR MOM ⊙

Have you ever stopped and tried to fathom the awesomeness of God? When I do, my blown up sense of self pops and shrivels much like a balloon after the party. Until, I am reminded that God has chosen me and He calls me specifically by name. We were created in His image. He knows everything there is about each and every one of us, the good, the bad and the ugly, and yet He still desires to get to know each person intimately.

Living in a rural area, I tend to forget just how many people there are in this vast world of ours. Whenever my husband and I venture out into the big city, I am once again reminded that I am but one of the million and billions of faces on this huge planet. Such thoughts always trigger simultaneous awe and humility. Because even with all of those millions of billions of faces, God still cares to know me. He wants to have a relationship with me. Yes me! *Why me?* God is so awesome, so powerful and yet He wants to know me, a mere guppy in the sea of so many.

He knows your name too. He aches to have a relationship with you. Spend time with God and cultivate the seeds of friendship. Experience the love He offers that surpasses all earthy understanding. Mom, He wants to know you and nourish your soul. *Get it* and get to know Him.

⏰ TIME FOR TEACHING ⏰
Read: Isaiah 40:21-26 and Psalm 139:13-16
God in His infinite everything wants to know you. Open your heart and get to know Him.

Making the First Move

*In your anger do not sin: Do not let the sun go down while you are
still angry, and do not give the devil a foothold.* Ephesians 4:26-27

My husband is angry with me. Why? Who knows? The point
is he is mad. We have barely spoken for days. I've tried to ap-
pease him with decent meals (which aren't my thing) and an
orderly home (which is difficult with four kids ambushing my
efforts) but nothing seems to help. I wish I knew what was bugging him. Heaven forbid I *ask*. That would mean breaking the
silence. No, he's the one that is mad; he needs to make the first
move to settle this conflict between us.

To be honest, I'm not quite the innocent victim I would like
you to believe. Gary and I are not much different when it comes
to conflict. When I'm upset, I too shut down. Our kids never
hear us argue, we just don't communicate. Though words may
never be spoken, a war rages within and as in all wars, there are
causalities, our kids. When war is raging with Dad, Mom's internal seething sets a mine field. My kids may not be aware but the
slightest miscalculation can set Momma off. Little things, which
normally wouldn't amount to much, cause unexpected explosive
behavior. Whoever happens to be in the line of fire becomes the
innocent victim in this war without words.

Now, please understand this is just a literary analogy. My husband and I do enjoy a wonderful marriage and the only blazing
firearms in my home are the popguns Grandma couldn't resist
gifting to my boys. Even so, there is occasionally trouble in paradise. Disagreements do arise. To end a conflict of this nature,
someone must speak. Someone must apologize. Someone must
make the first move. Love does just that.

In a recent sermon, one key phrase stuck with me: Love makes
the first move. This simple statement speaks profound truth.
Isn't that what God calls us to do? Even when we have been

wronged, sometimes to make it right, we need to step forward and make the first move. When you get right down to it, does it really matter whose fault it is anyway? Instead, what really matters is reconciliation. Love takes one giant step forward. The funny thing is, when I take that giant first step, my husband often reciprocates meeting me in the middle.

Christ made the first move. Before we were willing or even able to ask for forgiveness of our sins, He died on the cross to offer atonement for them. In Mel Gibson's movie, *The Passion of Christ*, one intense scene that stood out in my mind was when Christ literally placed Himself on the cross. He wasn't kicking or screaming and the soldiers didn't have to force Him down. He willingly placed Himself on the cross as a living sacrifice for you and me. Love makes the first move.

Later that day, Gary came home from work with a beautiful bouquet of flowers. He didn't say much, but took a step forward towards reconciliation. After dinner, when we finally had a moment alone, we sorted out our differences and worked our way back to paradise. When I've blown it with my kids, I need to take the initiative and apologize as well. Love unites, sin divides. To live as Christ, we must love and love always makes the first move.

☙ TIME FOR HIM ❧

Thank You Lord for the perfect example of love You gave us through Your Son. He made the first move and died for my sins. Help me to die to self so that I can love by His example. The relationships I have with my children and husband are far too important to allow hurt feelings to fester. Give me a heart that seeks reconciliation, asks for forgiveness, and is always willing to make the first move.

☙ TIME FOR MOM ❧

When disagreements divide your relationships, do you withdraw or explode? With my husband, I almost always withdraw, but with my kids I can be explosive (depending on the time of the month of course). Neither one are good options. But, as a rule, I believe it is best to hold the tongue lest it do damage. The tongue has an evil all of its own. If allowed to run amuck it can wreak a havoc that can only be repaired with much time, lots of flowers, and chocolate (the good stuff, not the cheap variety.)

Next time you are faced with a confrontation try to take a step back and emotionally remove yourself. I'm not saying this will be easy, but try it. Pray about the situation and ask God for discernment. Allow things to cool off a bit. Then, make the first move towards reconciliation. Try this even if you were the one that was wronged. "But, that's not fair," you moan. No one ever said life was fair. God's ways are not the world's ways. Sometimes we need to make a move that goes against our human nature in order to resolve the issue at hand. What's more important; restoring a broken relationship or saving face? Hmm…

You may be surprised at the results. Love softens. When you show love, the offending party can't help but be emotionally moved. Next time you find yourself on the battlefield, remember, love makes the first move. Not to attack but to surrender. Lovingly surrender and submit yourself to the enemy and see how the tide turns for the better.

🕐 TIME FOR TEACHING 🕐

Read: 1 Peter 4:8, Colossians 3:13-14, and 1 John 4:7-21

Christ commanded us to love one another and love always takes the initiative towards reconciliation.

DAY 5

He Spoke to Me!

*...the sheep listen to his voice. He calls his own sheep by name and
leads them out...and his sheep follow him because they know his voice.*
John 10:3-4

It was Good Friday, a solemn day. We had an evening service
and I was asked to lead the music in our little country church. As
the final strain of the last song rang in the air, the pastor came
forward and asked the congregation to bow their heads for a
moment of quiet. We were instructed to ask God what he would
like to say to each of us on this Good Friday.

Many thoughts flooded my mind at this simple request. Listening to God has always somewhat perplexed me. In my attempts to hear God, I always questioned whether the thoughts
that entered my mind were of my own making or if they really
were God speaking to my heart. I found it difficult to distinguish
that still small voice that I hear so much about. There was also a
part of me that feared what God would actually say. Would He
condemn me for all my many Mommy mess ups? Would He
ask me to do things that I didn't want to do? Would He say No
when I really wanted a Yes? All of these questions and feelings of
inadequacy raced through my mind in that one simple segment
of time.

Since I had just finished leading the singing, I was still positioned in front of everyone. I couldn't use my children as an
excuse to distract my attention. Briefly surveying the congregation to confirm that all heads were in fact bowed, I hesitantly
succumbed to the request and closed my eyes while lowering my
head as the lights dimmed.

Timidly, I posed the question, "Lord, what would you say to
me on this Good Friday?" Immediately my thoughts turned to
all of my failings at Motherhood and I scolded myself, "Get your
act together Judy!" But as quickly as the caustic command en-

tered my mind, another voice softly spoke to my heart. It simply stated, "I love You."

For a moment, time seemed to stand still as the words resonated in my mind. *I love you? Where did that come from? Did I hear correctly?* I questioned feeling a bit awkward yet moved. Opening my eyes to look up, I internally asked God, *Was that You, Lord?* A pregnant bubble of silence followed. Although I didn't hear a yes, something in my heart confirmed that it really was God whispering words of love in my ear.

Caught off guard by the intimacy of the moment, my face flushed as I suddenly became aware that others may be watching. I struggled to maintain my composure as a wave of emotion swept over me. I had felt anything but lovable that day and yet God whispered "I love you" to my heart. Looking up once again, I whispered back, "I love You too."

⏰ TIME FOR HIM ⏰

Lord, You are so wonderful. You speak to me in so many different ways. Sometimes it's a word whispered in my ear. At other times Your voice filters through the inspirational remarks of a friend. Your written Word is packed full of personal messages that seem penned to specifically pierce my heart. Help me to open myself up to You, recognize Your voice, and then respond to Your leading.

⏰ TIME FOR MOM ⏰

Wouldn't it be great if God continued to speak through burning bushes? It worked for Moses. Why can't God speak to modern Mom in the same way? I believe a bush that was not consumed by fire would surely attract my attention and make communication with God and life in general a whole lot easier.

The fact is, God only used a burning bush once and I doubt He will ever use it again. Our God is creative, imaginative, and requires us to step out in faith usually without all the answers so easily set before us. Although God might not literally use burning bushes to get our attention, He does send up a variety of smoke signals to get His message across.

Henry Blackaby outlines in his Bible study, *Experiencing God* that "God speaks by the Holy Spirit through the Bible, prayer, circumstances, and the church to reveal Himself, His purposes, and His ways."[6] It is not so much the how that is important. It is recognizing and responding to His voice that counts. We just need to trust God and open our hearts enough to listen. Take a moment to be quiet. Don't use your kids as an excuse. Even on the busiest of days, I bet if you ask God, He will grant you a few free minutes to seek Him. Ask God to reveal Himself to you. The amazing thing is, He will and when He does, you will know it. You can distinguish His voice. Remember, His sheep know His voice and they follow Him. Open yourself up to God. Ask Him to speak to you and then listen and recognize the Shepherd's voice. His words could be as simple as an "I love you." Oh, who could ask for a more beautiful message? Listen. Can you hear Him right now?

🕐 TIME FOR TEACHING 🕐
Read: John 8:47, and John 16:13
God wants to reveal Himself to you. Open up your heart to Him and simply listen. He could be speaking to you at this very moment.

Work Those Muscles

She sets about her work vigorously; her arms are strong for her tasks.
Proverbs 31:17

Yes, I am referring to exercise! Break a sweat! Work those muscles! "Ugh!" is the first response I generally hear when suggesting exercise and "When?" the second. Actually, come to think of it, these are *my* responses to the suggestion that I should do something more than just cozy up on the couch while *watching* my favorite aerobics' video. The thought of getting up and actually doing it, well, that just sounds kind of sweaty and as a rule this Mom does not like to sweat. On second thought, I do occasionally enjoy the perspiring promoting taste of hot Buffalo wings. Does that count? Maybe, NOT!

But, as I travel to speak to various Moms' groups, I have gleaned from their experience and yes, some of my own, that exercise really is a great time-out activity. Exercise promotes energy, how, I am not sure, but it does! When you exercise on a regular basis, not only do you feel and look better, your energy level is boosted as well. Hey, what busy Mom doesn't need that!

But, the question still remains, "When?" Sometimes you have to be creative in finding time to exercise during this busy season of life. But, it is possible. Some of the suggestions below involve working out with kids. You can also swap babysitting with friends or join a fitness center that offers babysitting for a small fee if not free. You can find the time if you put your mind to it. The benefits are enormous. Not only will you look better, you will feel better too.

When I refer to *work those muscles*, I am also referring to your mental capacities, which means give your brain a workout! Read something other than Dr. Seuss. Stretch your mind with something that expands your field of knowledge…something that doesn't rhyme…something that adds brains cells instead of taking them away. (I hate to break the news Ladies, but with each child you birth, you actually lose brain cells. Remember that finally push after your child was born. The doctor may have called it the placenta, but actually that was a portion of your brain that exited your body. This is true! I think? What was I just saying… see, too many kids!)

This week break a sweat. No, I am not talking about pulling out that spicy Chili recipe you have wanted to try. Exercise your body and mind. Who knows, this time-out might just move from your latest fad to your newest addiction.

TIME-OUT TIPS

Dust off the aerobics tapes! Pop in a tape at nap time and work up a sweat. This is a convenient and easy way to exercise.

Walk! Strap your kids in the stroller and take a walk. If you are an early riser get up before your family and take an early morning stroll. The inviting crack of dawn air is so refreshing. Try it!

Join a class! If at all possible join a fitness club or sign up at the local YMCA. Or take a class that stretches your mind. Babysitters and budgets need to be taken into consideration. But, if you can, get away to work-out mentally and physically.

Baby-ercise! When my kids where infants, I tried to incorporate them into my fat fighting routine. Strengthen arms by lifting your baby over your head. Place them on the floor and interact while doing push ups, scrunches, or other floor exercises. They love it and you will love the results.

Utilize little minutes! Our days are littered with little minutes of idleness. Whether we are waiting on the microwave or an appointment, we have an abundance of little pockets of time throughout the day. Utilize this time wisely. Do some knee bends, jog in place, or read. Use little minutes to squeeze in short work-out sessions for your mind and body.

The to-go bag! I always carry a small tote bag filled with different reading and writing materials. Whenever I have a few free minutes, I am prepared with something interesting to do.

Go the library or utilize the internet! Did you know that you can go online to search the library and check out books? (Now, I do realize that your library might not offer this option. But ask, often they do.) We have so many free resources available to expand our minds these days. Take advantage of them and do some research.

Work those muscles, both physical and intellectual. This type of time-out will not only give you a break from your kids, you will also become more physically fit and educationally well rounded.

The Ultimate Transformer

Therefore, if anyone is in Christ, he is a new creation; the old has gone, the new has come! 2 Corinthians 5:17

The latest boy toys are *Power Ranger Ninja Storm Triple Zord Morphin Transformers.* (I am not exaggerating! I copied the name from the box.) Sounds cool doesn't it? Simply rolling the words off the tongue sends a quick chill up the spine of any young boy. *Rescue Heroes* are another favorite of my younger son. Although the name *Rescue Hero* does not insight quite the same tingly effect, the song played on *Rescue Hero* videos does. My boys rave that it is "totally awesome!" Singing along even gives me a quick shoot of adrenaline that I too can take on and rescue the world.

Boy toys! With so much testosterone running amuck in my home, one can hardly take a step without tripping over these powerful plastic pieces.

As my two young sons soared their *Ninja Storm Blue Thunder Transforming* "whatever?" through the kitchen to save the world from the next mega-villain, the thought crossed my mind, *Why do my boys feel such a need to play with these action figures when they have me—MOM! I am the ultimate transformer and rescue hero?* With a single swoop, my kiss heals the bloodiest scabbed knee. I transform from cook, to housekeeper, to comforter, and counselor within seconds. I know it takes them much longer to transform their little powerful people into its various mega-manipulations. Just last night, I found myself washing a load of laundry, cooking a well-balanced meal, drawing a bath for my dirty duo, all while soothing a fussy baby, and instructing my daughter in the fine art of vacuuming. Impressive! Huh! I am much more than a transformer. I am a multi-manipulations master. *Boy, I am totally awesome!* I cheered myself on with a swift pat on the back.

Just as my ego was about to explode all over my beautiful birch kitchen cabinets, God gently brought me back to reality. He reminded me that without *His* transforming power in my life, I couldn't even leap the smallest building with a single bound. For it is only by *His* loving touch that I have been blessed with a wonderful family with which to share my many talents. It is by *His* grace that I have been transformed into a new creature by the shedding of *His* Son's blood.

Humbled, my thoughts drifted back to my life before... I'm embarrassed to even think about it. My selfish nature was in full swing back then. Going my own way I made a lot of mistakes, in fact, one could say I was a mega-mess. But then Jesus came along. He tugged at my heart until I couldn't resist any longer. His complete forgiveness white washed my past. He became my *rescue hero* and now daily transforms me into a Mom that can serve Him only through His divine strength. In my dreams, I am the ultimate transformer. But my juggling abilities pale in comparison to His transforming power and love.

As my boys rushed by once again saving the day from its most recent mega-villain, my thoughts turned towards them.

Today, my little men enjoy saving the world with your powerful plastic people. It is my prayer that some day you will meet the true ultimate transformer and allow Him to rescue you and by His perfect power and grace totally transform your life.

☺ TIME FOR HIM ☺

Lord, You are the ultimate life transformer. Just as one drop of dye completely colors a glass of water, one touch of Your hand dramatically transforms the lives of those that seek You. Thank You for being my rescue hero and transforming my life so completely. Without You, I am nothing. I pray that as I face the many multi-tasking occupations of Motherhood, You will continue to transform me into the Mom that You have purposed me to be.

☺ TIME FOR MOM ☺

Today's Moms wear a wide variety of hats. We are nurses, counselors, teachers, policewomen, interior designers, nutritionists, chefs, maids (not my favorite occupation).... The list goes on and on. Multi-tasking is a must for modern Mom. No matter how proficient we become at juggling, rescuing, and transforming into whatever the need of the moment requires, there is an ultimate transformer that surpasses our best performance. God transformed a forgotten shepherd boy into a mighty king with a heart that burned for Him. He revealed Himself to a harlot at a well and transformed her testimony to touch generations. He transformed a mismatched motley crew of fishermen to become fishers of men and revolutionize the world. He is a God that elevates the unlikely and has the power to completely transform any life from the darkest of pasts. All one needs is a willing spirit that says, "Yes Lord! Change me!"

Have you experienced His power? Have you allowed God to dramatically transform your life? It doesn't matter what you have done or how bad you have been; he can do a holy heart makeover with a mere touch of His hand.

Don't miss out on the exciting action packed adventure God has planned for your life. Be willing! Say yes! Allow God's superhuman touch and saving grace to rescue you and totally transform your life today.

🕐 TIME FOR TEACHING 🕐
Read: Acts 9:1-19 and Romans 12:2
If He can transform Saul's murderous rampage into a mighty ministry, just think what He can do for you.

DAY 2

Letting Go

...A time to hold on and another to let go.
Ecclesiastes 3:6 (The Message)

The pool was crowded, too crowded. *How is my son ever going to learn how to swim with all of these kids butting in, vying for the teacher's attention?* I thought to myself as the first chip gently fell from my shoulder. *Will, really "needs" to learn how to swim. That lake in back of the house scares me to death. I am so afraid that one of these days he will fall in and...* Shaking my head to banish the next thought, another chip plunked on the cement as waves of irritation rolled in.

Turning my attention back to Will my complaints increased. *Look at that! The teacher is never going to get to "my" son.* Leaning forward to toss a figurative lifesaver, I hesitated and then eased back with a sigh as the teacher's attention suddenly shifted towards my son.

There she goes, finally! I reassured, observing the teacher asking Will to dunk his head into the water...only to have him... What! Refuse?!

You can't be serious. Will what is wrong with you! The chips off my shoulder now lay in a huge heap next to my pool side lounge as the temperature of the sunny afternoon peaked past 100. Actually, I believe that was my temper burning. I could not comprehend how this son of mine could so defiantly cop an attitude when what he really needed to do was learn how to swim!

Maintaining control was no longer an option. Compelled to fix this situation, I abruptly stood up and belted towards the pools edge. Halfway there, a sudden awareness of my "public" surroundings caused me to second guess my approach. *I better tone it down.* I corrected, smoothing back my ruffled Mother hen feathers. Slowing my stride I put on a "happy" face as I quickly approached my son determined to coach him back to submission.

Mustering up my sweetest Mommy voice, I gently encouraged, "Put your head in the water, William. You can do it!" Then without thinking my tone hardened, "Will, you've done it before, re—mem—ber!" I emphasized each syllable as my eyes now blazed.

As Will looked up, I noticed that his expression was not one of "Thanks for the tip Mom." Instead, his hazel blues returned a look of, "Mom, leave me alone!" Just as my stance stiffened, prepared to retaliate and set this boy straight, I was met with a similar evil eye from the teacher. Taken aback, my face flushed. Then with tsunami strength the realization hit. *I have just crossed the line into a place that Moms should not go.* The harsh reality of it all sunk like a dead weight in my heart.

Begging my pardon, I slithered back to the safety of that pool side lounge, picking up the chips along the way and returning them to my shoulder—where they should have stayed all along. *How could I be so stupid?* I chastised myself embarrassed by my indiscretion. Breathing in a cleansing breath, I chained myself to my sideline seat allowing my son to sink or swim on his own. Ugh!

Although we resist the notion, the whole point of mothering is letting go. We teach, correct, encourage, and nurture, only to some day *let go* of our little masterpieces. In fact, mothering is a series of *letting go* moments. From the first time you relinquish the care of your precious newborn to the arms of a babysitter, to letting your son go potty by himself in the men's room, to handing over the car keys with a cringe, to driving him to college and holding your breath as you wave goodbye. Letting go! It is the most heart wrenching part of Mothering.

God calls us to *let go.* Proverbs 22:6 reads, "Train up a child in the way he should *go.*" There is no mention of Mom tagging along. It says GO! Ouch! Now I do realize that I am taking this verse somewhat out of context. But, the simple truth remains that a Mother's job is to work herself out of a job and that involves the painful art of letting go. And letting go involves trust.

Allowing the golden rays of the afternoon sun melt away my fears, I lifted my sweet William up in prayer.

He's in Your hands God. Help him to learn how to swim! With each roll of the tide I pray that my son will always be able to keep his head above water and not just survive but thrive as he walks or rather swims with You.

Today, I *let go* and trust enough to *let God.*

☺ TIME FOR HIM ☺

Lord, why is it so painful to let go of my babies? The urge to rescue is often overwhelming. Sometimes I need take a step back and allow my children to learn from experience. Give me wisdom to know when to hold on and the courage to let go.

☺ TIME FOR MOM ☺

Are you a helicopter Mom? Do you hover over your children waiting to rescue? Maybe, it is time to learn to *let go.*

We tend to do a lot of fishin' living out in the country. Catching *the big one* is an exciting event. Usually, we clean our catch for a family fish fry. Sometimes, however, we release the prize, to allow it to grow up a little more. Then there are times when the kids and I enjoy watching the fish swim from the sidelines of a paddleboat, marveling at their dexterity in the water.

Mom, raising kids is a lot like fishin'. There are times we need to catch 'em and keep 'em; take care of our minnows until they are ready to do on their own. Then there are times we need to catch 'em, teach 'em, and release 'em back into the pond to experience freedom with Mom's fishnet close at hand. Then there are the times, which take the most restraint, we need to just sit in the boat with a sense of pride as we watch our guppies mature and make it on their own.

Whichever level of fishin' you are experiencing right now, remember, God has entrusted His children, yes, *His* children into your care for a season. As God trusts you, you must also trust Him.

Pray for your kids. Place them in God's hands and then trust Him! He will guide you and give you wisdom as you journey through all the *letting go* moments of Motherhood.

⏱ TIME FOR TEACHING ⏱

Read: Genesis 22:1-12, 1 Samuel 1:27-28, and Exodus 2:1-10

God challenged Abraham with the ultimate letting go test and he passed. What grade would you receive on a similar challenge?

DAY 3

Reflections

These commandments that I give you today are to be upon your hearts. Impress them on your children. Talk about them when you sit at home and when you walk along the road, when you lie down and when you get up. Deuteronomy 6:6-7

At four months old, Joseph's baby babble is music to my ears. I love it! Words cannot express the exploding joy I feel simply by listening to my little guy talk. It is so addicting. It's like eating potato chips. One chip leads to another; you can't just stop. So, like a junkie, I encourage Joseph to talk to me. I tickle, tease, whatever it takes. I just gotta have those sweet smiles, baby coos, delectable giggles, and best of all, baby talk. Delicious!

One day, as I watched my eight-year-old daughter enjoying a quiet moment of communication with her baby brother, I noticed, to my surprise, that she used the exact same terminology with the exact same voice inflection to coax her brother to talk as I did. It was a scary "look in the mirror" kind of a moment to think that my daughter imitated my actions so exactly.

As I reflected to other not so Kodak moments, a shiver ran up my spine. *What other behaviors are my children copying when I least expect it?* I flushed. Hmm…

We would like to think that "Do as I say and not as I do," really does work. But the hard truth is—it doesn't. Our children learn far more from what we do than what we say. For example, I can reprimand using all the appropriate language but if my tone is angry, all my children actually perceive is that it is O.K. to lash out in anger. My actions completely overshadow my words. Ouch! They say actions speak louder than words. I hate to admit it, but the old adage rings painfully true.

It is truly terrifying to think that I, in my humanness, have such a strong impact on how my children learn to handle life. I am not always a "good Mom" or even a "good person." It's terrible difficult to be *on* 24/7. But that's what Moms do. All day little eyes are watching and recording our responses to all types of situations, good or bad. Sometimes I just want to hide and take a break from the responsibility.

On the other hand, I see all the wonderful opportunities that I have to positively shape my children. Hopefully, by catching me with my Bible open and spending time in prayer, they will see that it is important to take time-out for God. Hopefully, by making a meal for the friend in need, they will catch a glimpse of the value of service. Hopefully, by being encouraging instead of constantly criticizing they will learn to handle others with care. Hopefully, there is a glimmer of good that outshines all of the bad I would rather erase.

Turning my thoughts back to today's observation, I reflected with a brief moment of prayer.

Thank you Lord that today my daughter mirrored a positive trait that she has learned by my example. Help me to always honor You by setting an example for my children that is pleasing in Your sight.

☺ TIME FOR HIM ☺

Thank You, Lord, for reminding me of the powerful influence my behavior has on my children. Please forgive me when I fail. Give me the power to be the positive example that You intend for me to be. Thank You for sending Jesus to be my role model. By Your strength, I pray that my life always reflects Him.

☺ TIME FOR MOM ☺

Do you see yourself in your children? It's like looking in the mirror in more ways that one isn't it? I can't tell you how many times I have overheard my oldest playing policeman to her younger siblings using the same staccato tone and curt criticisms that I have emulated. It's not always a pretty picture. Then there are times, that I catch a glimpse of a positive trait mirrored through their actions and words. What a wonderful pat on the back.

What kind of example are you setting for your kids? The next time you find yourself in a heated situation, take a step back and try to see yourself through your child's eyes. What kind of role model are you? Are they learning self-control or out-of-control? If you fail, which happens, go to your kids and ask for forgiveness. Set an example that says when I make a mistake, I take responsibility.

Most importantly, let your kids catch you with your Bible open. As I write my stories and delve into scripture, I have noticed that my daughter has gained a sense of pride in knowing that Mom is on an important mission to try and share God's Word.

We can teach our kids to be honest, kind to others, and do good deeds. These are all wonderful attributes. But, being a "good person" won't get you a ticket into heaven. Saying, "Yes!" to Jesus and daily seeking Him is what God requires. You can't take your possessions with you, but, you can take your kids. Set an example that teaches your kids that even though you aren't perfect, by God's grace, you are forgiven. Demonstrate a passion for God's Word and a desire to serve Him. You have to live it and prayerfully by your lead they will live it too.

You can do it Mom! Be a positive role model for your children. Set an example that they will strive to become. Remember, little eyes are always watching. Give them something worthy to watch.

TIME FOR TEACHING

Read: Colossians 1:10-12, 2 Corinthians 3:18, and Psalm 19:14

Jesus set an example for how He wants us to live. Live a life that is pleasing to Him.

DAY 4

Digging for Gold

For where your treasure is, there your heart will be also.
Matthew 6:21

It has become a tradition in the Crawford home to celebrate birthdays with treasure hunts. I make up clues and then hide them around the yard. It is great fun and often the highlight of the party.

While cleaning up after one such party, treasure envy crept into my thoughts. Begrudgingly picking up the neglected candy wrapper spoils, the penetrating question, "Where is *my* treasure?" needled its way to the forefront of my mind. I guess the afterglow of the festivities left me lacking as a different sort of party emerged—a pity party. It went something like this... *All I ever do is pick-up after these kids. When is it my turn? When do I get to have a little fun and actually find some sort of treasure? At least something better than these "golden" candy wrappers that my kids can't seem to remember to throw away in the trash can—where they belong!* I hesitated momentarily as Mommy guilt began to unload. Consciously choosing to ignore the warning, I continued on and on... My pity party was in full swing.

Sometimes it is difficult to catch the glimmer of gold in these not-so-golden years of Mothering. It seems that the only fortune I find is some neglected spare change left behind in dirty pants pockets as I'm sorting laundry. The only golden nuggets I uncover are the kind found in my toddler's stinky diaper. Last week, as I lingered on the phone, my little guy happened upon a box of corn flakes. Through the course of my engaging conversation, he managed to sneak past me and disseminate the entire box leaving a trail that traveled through three rooms. The flakes were golden all right but not the kind of gold I was hoping for.

My complaints mounted adding weight to the load of laundry I struggled to carry up the stairs. As I plodded along rehearsing each grievance with each added step, something caught my eye shifting my focus. My once immaculate white walls (well maybe not immaculate but white just the same) were now refurbished with a new sort of décor accent. As I leaned in closer to discern their origin it became apparent that my stairway was redecorated with tiny pink hand prints. Ugh! I soon discovered that a trail of the fresh rosy markings also littered light switches, windows, and just about any once clean surface. A heavy sigh of exhaustion escaped as another uninvited annoyance crashed my pity party.

Just as I was about to scold the older siblings for not catching their younger brother sooner, a faint recollection surfaced and caught my tongue from flapping more venting. I remembered a recent prayer request for a young infertile couple. In their attempts to adopt a child, they were now faced with a heavy financial burden and lots of red tape. It occurred to me that this want-to-be Mother's perspective on the pastel prints that lined my walls would sharply contrast from mine. Instead of viewing them as a nuisance, she might welcome their presence. In fact, she might even frame a few as masterful works of art.

In that moment, the brilliance of gold magically materialized. Only it wasn't the type of gold I thought I was seeking. I always imagined that real treasure was in a bigger house, a nicer car, or even in some sort of honored achievement. This was a different kind of gold, a diamond in the rough with lasting value and it was right in front of me all along; I just needed to follow the clues to find it.

Capturing the sticky finger bandit, I stretched his messy hand out in mine. Looking up into the deepness of his baby blues, my little guy let out a mischievous giggle that inspired a delightful rush of love. *I believe I've found it! Gold that is! Yes my son. You are my treasure!*

☙ TIME FOR HIM ☙

Thank You, Lord, for the gift of children. Things of this world easily distract me from the most important. Help me to always have eyes to see and the heart to appreciate the true treasure in my life.

⏰ TIME FOR MOM ⏰

Where is your treasure? What do you value most in life? When asked these questions, I believe most of us would respond that our family is most important. And I would hope that many of you would say that your relationship to God is highly valued as well. But, when you get right down to the nitty gritty of it all, is that *really* where your heart is?

As I write these words, the jingle bells of Christmas announce the approaching holiday. My kitchen counter is littered with ad upon ad of blow-out bargains luring me into the buying season. I can't help but wonder at what point have we crossed the line? When does the gift become more important than the giver? By allowing our children to get everything on their wish list, what message are we sending? Is their treasure in the *treasure*, Santa's maxed out credit card, or is it in the magic of Christmas, time with friends and family, the awe of our Savior's birth?

So, I am back to my initial question, where does your treasure lie? Is it in a bigger house, high tech toys, or a sportier car? Or is it in prestigious positions, climbing the later of success, lengthy titles after your name? (I mean something better than expert bottom wiper!) Where does your treasure lie? When is enough...enough? By allowing ourselves every indulgence under the sun, are we storing up treasures of this earth or treasures in heaven? It's a fuzzy line, isn't it?

This week, take an inventory of your heart. Ask God to reveal where your true treasure lies. If you have bought into the excessiveness of this world, map out a plan to refocus your values, have a garage sale, or better yet donate what you really don't need to someone that really does need it. Slim down your spending and soon true treasures will materialize right before your eyes. Store up this type of treasure, the kind with lasting value, treasure that will live on in your heart for an eternity.

⏰ TIME FOR TEACHING ⏰

Read: Matthew 6:19-21, Ecclesiastes 5:15, and Ecclesiastes 2:8-11
Store up treasures in heaven, treasures that last forever.

DAY 5

Songs in the Night

But no one says, "Where is God my Maker that gives songs in the night..." Job 35:10

Weaning my son of our nightly rendezvous' has been difficult to say the least. My pediatrician hinted that the reason he wasn't sleeping through the night yet was because room service was a little too good. Well, I guess he's right. I have no excuses... except that it's easier. And in the middle of the night, easy is about all I am up too. On the other hand, I have to admit, I have become a slave to my son. Recently, determined to take back control, I have let Joseph cry himself back to sleep. And guess what, it was working!

Tonight, however, was different. Why? Because Joseph was coming down with a cold and as any good Mother knows all rules change when that thermometer peaks past 100. So, when that familiar cry woke me up around 1 a.m. I just didn't have the heart to let him cry it out. But still, I really didn't want to break a winning record either? Teetering back and forth, I finally decided to just rub his back a little with the hopes that it he could settle himself back to sleep without me picking him up. Recognizing Mom's touch, his restlessness subsided. I in turn silently celebrated as I watched my son's breathing slowly settle back into its peaceful rhythmic flow.

Soaking in the solitude, a key phrase from Sunday's sermon echoed in the corners of my mind, "songs in the night." The words seemed so profound and poetic. My pastor explained that the intent of the verse was not a literal song during the midnight hour. A song in the night is when you sense God's presence in the middle of your darkest pain. It is when a shimmer of joy and peace momentarily resonates in a broken heart. Just as my gentle touch calmed my fussy hurting child, God caresses our hearts with a simple soothing melody in the midst of our suffering.

Simply put, He is that song in the night.

I have experienced this uncanny quiet through the storm several times. When tragedy strikes and I feel that I should be falling apart, yet there is a thread of God's presence that mysteriously holds me together and offers hope.

A friend of mine recounts a similar experience. An unexplained fainting spell prompted a series of medical tests, some of which were quite serious and even involved minor surgery. Through each grueling procedure she could sense God's presence overflow her apprehensive heart. To paraphrase Sheri's words, "Judy, I can't explain it, but I knew that no matter what the outcome, God would see me through. He has provided perfect peace and calm through every unknown that lies ahead." I knew exactly what Sheri struggled to pinpoint; it was that unexplainable peace that passes all understanding described in Philippians 4:7. God was her song in the night.

God promises, "Never will I leave you…" (Hebrews 13:5) He will be right at our side through whatever life throws our way. But, in order for God to come to us, we need to first go to Him. Proverbs 8:17 reads, "I love those who love me, and those who seek me find me." Sheri was seeking God. I know she was. And she found Him whispering a song of peace to her anxious heart.

Unfortunately, for many of us our first response to trouble is not always a seeking of God. Instead we try to fix things on our own or fill the void with stuff. Food, shopping, and people are three popular void fillers that I have used in the past. All I'm left with are hefty hips, a bigger balance on my credit card, and friends that soon turn a deaf ear to my tiresome tales. There is an empty-ness in the heart of Mom. Often, we search for peace and contentment in all the wrong places. If only we would open ourselves up to God, his presence would fill the deep yearning in our hearts.

Unfortunately tonight, my touch did not have the same comforting effect on my son as I had hoped. He woke up again, only this time he somehow managed to crawl out of his diaper and wet himself and his entire crib. What a mess! Haphazardly cleaning it up I gave in and let Joseph sleep in our bed. (Sometimes, you gotta do what you gotta do.)

Snuggling my son close, I too, felt God's gentle arms wrap themselves around me. He reassured me that wet beds and sleepless nights are but a season of life that will pass all too quickly. I know that God will always be with me granting an odd peace through whatever problems I face. He is my sweet song in the dark night.

TIME FOR HIM

Thank You for being my song in the night. It is amazing that a mere glimpse of Your presence can make everything right when on the surface it appears so wrong. You are wonderful and mysterious. Forgive me when I try to fill the void with other things. Help me to always have a heart that seeks You first.

TIME FOR MOM

Have you ever experienced a song in the night? Have you felt God's presence in the midst of your pain? It is an uncanny revelation. When all seems wrong and on the surface it is, somehow a glimmer of odd peace works its way into your heart and calms your restless spirit. Mom, this is the Holy Spirit, the great comforter speaking to you. Do you know His voice?

Next time tragedy strikes, don't succumb to despair. Don't try to fill the void with stuff. These substitutes only lead to a deeper emptiness. Instead, seek God. He can handle any and all of your trouble. When you lay your burdens at His feet, He will turn the tide and whisper peace to your troubled heart. Listen! He may be singing to you right now. Can you hear Him?

TIME FOR TEACHING

Read Psalm 42:8, John 14:27, and John 16:33

God never promised that life would be easy. He did promise, however, that He would be there with you. Open yourself up to Him and listen. He may be singing a sweet comforting melody to you at this very moment.

Stay Connected

If one falls down, his friend can help him up. But pity the man who falls and has no one to help him up! Ecclesiastes 4:10

Mothering can be a lonely job. I know that sounds ridiculous when Moms by nature have multiple children attached to various parts of their bodies at any given time of day. But it's true. Mothering can be a very lonely job. Though our kids talk, talk, talk our ears off. (My four-year-old is going through a rather talkative stage right now.) Sometimes we need to converse with someone, anyone, that doesn't end every other word with a long "e." (Mommy, nappy, potty…shall I continue) And as much as we love our men, they really can only handle so many spoken words in a day. That is why we need women—female friends that will hopefully serve up a hefty dose of encouragement when we need that extra shot in the arm to get through the day.

The problem is, the busyness of everyday life with kids does not always allow much extra time for Moms to foster friendships. But, that is exactly what we need to do—to *survive*. We need to sow and cultivate the seeds of friendship. But, in order to have friends you need to first be a friend, and that means intentionally taking steps to initiate relationships with other women.

This week take some time-out to stay connected. I can't think of a better way to recharge your Mommy battery than to enjoy a good conversation with a cherished friend. Connect with your friends and reconnect with your peace of mind.

TIME-OUT TIPS
Pray about it! If you are having a hard time connecting with other women, pray about it. I did this. God answers all kinds of prayers. If you give Him a chance, He will open the door for you to bond with that special friend during this season of life.

Phone a friend! This sounds so simple. But sometimes we get so involved at home that we forget to make that phone call and stay connected.

Join a Mom's group! If you find it difficult to meet other Moms, locate a Mom's group in your area and join. Check out *MOPS* (Mothers of Preschoolers)! Go to www.mops.org to get more information and locate a *MOPS* group near you. Living in a rural community, I didn't have this option. So I started my own Moms group. My M.I.L.K. (Mothers, Infants, Little Kids) group has now meet for over ten years. What a blessing!

Be a friend! In order to have friends, you need to first be a friend. Take the initiative and invite a Mom and her kids over for a play time. You will enjoy your time together and your kids just might form new friendships of their own.

Don't forget to write! The written word has become blasé in our hyper speed generation of e-mail. Take time-out to write a letter or send a card. What a thrill to open the mailbox and find something other than junk mail or bills. Take advantage of snail mail and just maybe someone will reciprocate back to you.

E-mail a friend! I have several friends I call my "E" friends. We e-mail back and forth on a regular basis. This is a great way to cultivate friendships at any given time of day.

Plan a ladies' night out! Gather up a few girlfriends and go out on the town without kids. How freeing and refreshing. Do dinner, shop, and then top off the evening with dessert! Escape for an evening of food, friendship, and FUN!

Start a book club! In the summer, several friends of mine get together to read and discuss a chosen book. It's a little chaotic with all of our kids running around. But, the older children help out with the younger ones and somehow it works. This is a great way to develop friendships and your mind at the same time.

Take time-out to form friendships. How better to navigate this wonderful Mothering journey than with a close friend at your side. Next time you feel like pulling out your hair, phone a friend instead. She can help you refocus and may even have a few tips to offer on how to handle your latest kid challenge. Nourish your friendships and they will nourish you.

DAY 1

Only a Mom...

This is love: not that we loved God, but that he loved us and sent his Son as an atoning sacrifice for our sins. 1 John 4:10

Lately, feeding my little guy has become quite a challenge. Nothing seems to help. If I pretend that the spoon is a jet plane attempting to land in his mouth, he instinctively starts bombing my efforts with a quick jerk of the head or swipe of the hand sending my edible cargo everywhere except where it is supposed to be—in his mouth! So, in order to feed him his *scrumptious* lunch consisting of savory butternut squash, I sat him on my lap to better control his sabotaging ploys. Tilting his head back slightly to improve my aim, I gave myself a quick high five as my first plane landed safely. Swirling the squash in his mouth, his eyes danced with playfulness. Just as I was about to instruct him to swallow, he burst out a breath that colored my white T-shirt with a spray of orange goop. Yuck! What a mess!

The incident took me back to a conversation at a recent ladies' night out. After sharing all of our latest messy kid stories, we concluded that *only a Mom* would willfully put herself in the stinky sticky line of fire out of love for her children. *Only a Mom* would intentionally insert her finger just inside a diaper to see if it was poopy. *Only a Mom* would allow herself to be spit-up on over and over again and not think much of it. *Only a Mom* would put her hands out in front of her sick child to catch his vomit. Now, all things considered, there is a hidden agenda of salvaging carpet behind our efforts to catch throw-up. Ulterior motives set aside, Moms still suffer severe grossness out of love for their children.

A few months ago, my sister, who also has four small children, shared her latest gruesome tale. All in one morning, her potty training daughter pooped her pants, her son threw-up in the car, and her new baby not only spit-up all over her and the carpet, he let it loose on her shirt as she changed his diaper. She had spent the day immersed in a mass of body fluids, desperately trying to clean up each new mess her kids lay at her feet.

Yes, *only a Mom* would put up with all the smelly secretions of raising kids. Why? The answer is simple. We love our kids.

It's fun to joke about all the things we Moms go through… But, the truth is, if we were really honest, we would have to admit that we put God through much worse every single day. Ouch! That hurts! Actually, I'm sure that was exactly what Jesus was thinking as He willingly laid Himself upon that cross, as the nails penetrated the palms of His hands. Ouch, is putting it lightly. It was my sin that nailed Jesus to that Calvary tree. My sin pounded the nails into His innocent hands. He bore the burden of my sin, my stinky sloppy sin, why? He did it because He loves His kids and I am one of those kids.

Turning back to my messy boy, a reflective smile warmed my face. It feels good to be loved like that. To know that even though I am a mess, (in more ways than one—just look at this T-shirt!) God still loves me!

As I bent down to wipe my son's runny nose on my shirt, (Be honest! You've done it too. Haven't you?) I realize that God calls me to willfully endure the repulsive stickiness of raising kids. He sacrificed His Son as the penalty for my sins; the least I can do is sacrifice my T-shirt for my son's snotty nose.

Just as *only a Mom* will eagerly kiss her runny nosed child on the lips, *only God* can love me in spite of my failings. When I humble myself at His feet, He will wipe up the many messes I make each day. *Only God* can clean me up and still allow me to be used for His service, even when it is as simple as sacrificing a squash stained T-shirt to wipe a runny nose.

☺ TIME FOR HIM ☺

Dear Lord, just like my children, I too am often a mess. Thank You, Lord, for accepting me just as I am. Please forgive me. Clean me up and help me to start each day fresh through You.

⏰ TIME FOR MOM ⏰

Been there! Done that! Am I right? You don't have to be a Mom for very long to experience the sloppy secretions *only a Mom* is called to endure. Basically, kids are a mess! After lunch I snuck into the pantry to retrieve a piece of chocolate from my stash. For some reason I felt the strange inclination to share.

"Joseph, would you like some chocolate?" I quizzed as he greedily nodded yes.

"Are you worthy?" I questioned measuring up his chocolate sharing status.

You have to understand, this was *my* chocolate—Mom's special stash—a step up from your run of the mill chocolate bar. Simply put, it was *the good stuff.*

Sizing up my messy son, I concluded that he was not, in fact, worthy of such an indulgence. He had leftovers from lunch all over his shirt, he was still wearing his pajamas, and even worse, I knew that at the young age of four, he had not yet developed the proper palette to truly appreciate the creamy smooth texture of the chocolate I held in my hand.

But, guess what, I gave it to him anyway.

Mom, I hate to be the one to break the news to you, but you aren't worthy either. You're a mess! Just look at yourself in the mirror, what a mess! Now before you get all huffy on me, you need to realize that I am a mess too! We are all messes!

But, guess what, God offers the gift of eternal life to us anyway. (...which is sweeter than even the finest chocolate!)

Today, find peace in the knowledge that you are acceptable just as you are. God loves you! There is nothing you can do to win His love. It is a free gift. Accept it! Say yes and invite Jesus to live within your heart.

⏰ TIME FOR TEACHING ⏰

Read: 1 Kings 3:16-28, Ephesians 3:17-19, and Romans 8:38-39
Just as only a Mom would give up her son so that he might live; only God would willfully sacrifice His Son so that you might live.

DAY 2

Get a Grip

So do not fear, for I am with you; do not be dismayed, for I am your
God. I will strengthen you and help you; I will uphold you with my
righteous right hand. Isaiah 41:10

My life is a foreboding melody. Can you hear it? There it is again.

Duh, duh, duh, du—da duh, du—da duh! Can't you hear it? O.K. now I do realize that my terrifying tune may not translate well without the proper pitch inflection. But listen, I bet if you try hard enough, you can hear it. This time think *Star Wars* and Darth Vader and I think you will get it. Duh, duh, duh, du—da duh, du—da duh! Aha! You heard it! Didn't you?

Finally, someone else can feel my pain. Someone else can commiserate the fear and dread this perpetual melody is causing. Everywhere I go it lurks in the shadows, taunting me with its dark ominous flow. It's in my mini-van as we travel down the road running errands, it fades into the serenity of my kitchen, it even whispers in my ear as I rock my youngest to sleep. The unending impending doom is quite nerve-racking. If this goes on much longer I believe my frayed nerves just might snap.

Whatever happened to the perky, optimistic, "I love you…you love me, were such a happy family…" Purple dinosaur days are pre-historic in my home. In its place my *Star Wars* crazed youngest dutifully hums, drums, and strums this sinister song until I am forever feeling numb.

Fear, for some of us fear is a way of life. Just as this foreboding melody constantly lurks in the background of my life, fear's grip holds tightly to its victims paralyzing them from living life.

It's easy to hold on to fear when you are a Mom. I have a lot of fears. Here's a quick checklist of just a few. Maybe you can relate.

I fear that my propensity to badger my children might somehow permanently damage their self esteem.

I fear that my four-year-old will not learn to wipe his own bottom before he enters Kindergarten and the silence when I come home on the first day I drop him off.

I fear that I might lose my purse, or keys, or both.

I fear bad hair days and bounced checks.

I fear the scale at the doctor's office might actually be accurate.

I fear lightening will strike this computer, maybe even while I am typing—now that's a scary thought.

Wow! I just realized that as I am now typing—right now—the foreboding theme is literally playing in the background as my older son quietly occupies himself on a *Star War's* game on the playstation. Now that's really scary! No, that's eerie!

Then there are the fears that I hesitate to even express. Because I fear that if I breathe life into the words then somehow they might take shape and actually come true. Fear, it really is paralyzing.

These fears threaten to strangle until I am reminded of what fear actually is.

FEAR = False—Evidence—Appearing—Real.

That's all it is. And when you add God into that equation suddenly fear doesn't seem so fearful after all.

As my son clicks off the T.V. and my youngest happens by singing a new song (Thank heavens!) I realize that my foreboding melody is just that, a simple melody and not a theme in my life.

I have been known to tell others to "Get a grip!" (In a humorous sort of way mind you.) When it comes to fear, I believe this flippant phrase rings truth. We shouldn't allow fear to grip us. Instead *get a grip* on fear. But, to do that you need to first *get a grip* on God!

☻ TIME FOR HIM ☻

Dear God, I humbly bow before You out of fear, respect, and awe. Help me to feel Your presence in my life. Guide me as I learn to have more faith in You and less fear of things outside my control.

☻ TIME FOR MOM ☻

Do you have issues with fear? I believe we all do at some level. In fact, some fear is actually healthy. My son, William, enjoys living life on the edge. He fearlessly walks the fence, sometimes literally, as I breathlessly caution while he carelessly throws all caution to the wind. A good dose of fear could do him a little good.

Some fear is appropriate, healthy, and warranted. Over and over the Bible calls us to fear the Lord. This type of fear involves humility, respect, and an awareness of the proper order of how things out to be. We need this type of fear.

Then there are times that we allow fear to get out of hand. When unmerited fear looms into the domain of lack of faith, we need to step back and reconsider our emotions.

Whatever kind of fear you may be experiencing right now, know that God is there. He is there as you humbly bow before Him out of reverence, respect and yes, fear. And He is there with you as you *get a grip* on the day to day fears of Motherhood. Lean on Him. Trust in Him. *Get a grip* on God and He will hold your hand as you *get a grip* on fear!

⏰ TIME FOR TEACHING ⏰
Read: 1 Peter 5:6-7, Proverbs 19:23, and Psalm 56:3-4
Put fear in its proper place and suddenly fear losses its grip on you.

DAY 3

Just Give Me a Little P__ce!

Be still and know that I am God... Psalm 46:10

"Yes Joseph, I will be with you in a..." I absentmindedly re-marked staring at the blank screen while attempting to formulate my next thought.

"What? Sure, whatever, you can have a cookie; just keep it off the carpet." The tension now rising up my back settled in my shoulders pulsating at the base of my neck. The computer keys rested beneath my fingertips waiting...waiting...

Suddenly, the breakout of a brawl demanded my immediate attention. With a quick jerk of my head, I yelled out a crisp reprimand, "Will, leave your brother alone! Adam, be nice!" Pound, pound, pound my head throbbed from the strain of maintaining some sort of focus with all the chaos running amuck around me.

"What's that...dinner? Didn't we just eat?" Glancing down at my wristwatch the shock of 7 P.M. registered. *I guess it is time for dinner.*

Clicking down on the save tab, the irony of it all slapped me in the face. *What have I saved? Nothing, absolutely nothing! How am I ever going to write a book with this constant noise? Everyone wants a piece of Mom. Well, there's nothing left, no more pieces to go around.* My thoughts exploded as I stomped my way up to the kitchen...again!

Debating my dilemma, a light bulb flipped on in my head. *I think we need to have a family meeting.* I reasoned while formulating the speech that would set them all straight. Popping in the frozen popcorn shrimp and fries, I hastily set the table, calculating my family's response to the plan I was about to set in motion. *Finally, they will understand my point of view and maybe, just maybe they will leave me be so I can have the quiet I need to write this book.* The tension in my neck momentarily subsided as a thread of hope weaved its way into my thoughts.

Gathering around for our family meal I quickly commanded everyone's attention and began my rehearsed declaration of how things needed to change…or else!

"Now I realize that all of you could really care less about Mom's book. But, it is important to me and therefore it *needs* to be important to you. All day long I have Joseph talking my ear off and then you kids come home from school and I have this constant fighting in the background. How can anyone think nevertheless write with all of this noise! You need to understand this. If my book flops than I will fall into a deep dark depression and that does affect you. Because if Mom is depressed, trust me, you too will be depressed. I will make sure that you all feel my…

It was at this point that my husband had the audacity to snicker. Yes, snicker! Then the kids started to chuckle. Yes, chuckle! Soon contagious rolls of laughter bounced off the walls as I sat there dumbfounded by their obvious lack of concern for my plight. Then it happened, as much as I fought it, the hint of a smile made its way to the corners of my mouth and I let out a giggle or two, myself.

Peace and quiet seems to be a rare commodity when you have multiple people living in the same confined space. Everyone wants a *piece* of Mom when all Mom wants is a little *peace*. In as much as we do need to enjoy our families and all the commotion that goes along with that gift, we also need to balance the scales with moments of peace and solitude. Quiet to connect with God and quiet to connect with self.

Later that evening, I snuck back downstairs eager to click a few keys on the computer, only to hear the familiar stomp on the stairs of kids trailing behind. Confident that my talk had impacted my family, I opened my word document and proceeded to type when…

"Mom, can you give me my spelling words?" Will questioned anticipation written all over his face.

"Mom, come look at this." Adam peaked out of his bedroom awaiting my prompt arrival.

"Mom…

With a heavy sigh, I maneuvered my mouse to shut down the

computer for the night. *Someday, there will be peace. Someday, the incessant noise that reverberates throughout the walls of this home will take up a new residence in the walls of their homes as they each break away to start families of their own. Someday, I will have my peace. Until then, I guess for tonight, there still are a few pieces left to go around.*

☻ TIME FOR HIM ☻

Lord, thank You for the gift of family. Help me to balance the chaos of kids with moments of quiet. I pray that You would open up peaceful pockets of time in my hectic schedule. Help me to recognize these opportunities and use them wisely to re-nourish my parched spirit.

☻ TIME FOR MOM ☻

Peace, the word itself sounds so appealing, so comforting...so peaceful. As much as Moms would love to have a little peace, our children, who have yet to learn to spell, would also like to have a little piece—a piece of Mom that is. Such is life. Everyone is constantly pulling at us from every given direction, wanting a piece when in actuality there are really only so many pieces to go around.

Currently my parents are visiting. As we lingered over breakfast I noticed that my Mother's hands have developed a slight tremor in her old age. As my concerned Dad quizzed her about this new development, I quickly added my two-cents. "Dad, Mom has raised six kids; I believe her nerves are shot!" My Mom has given away so many pieces over the years; there is hardly a piece left. Yet still, the peace on her face tells me that somehow it was all worth while.

We should embrace all the craziness that goes along with raising a family. But still, we also need to balance our lives with moments of peace and quiet.

Mom, do you have a quiet time in your day, a few uninterrupted moments to pray, or think, or just be? The problem is, when those moments arrive, and yes we do occasionally have them, we tend to fill the void of quiet by turning on the radio or television. Take some time to enjoy the quiet. Resist the urge to fill in the gaps with background noise. Instead breathe in moments of silence. As William Penn once said, "True silence is the rest of the mind. It is to the spirit what sleep is to the body nourishment and refreshment."[7] Today, feed yourself a healthy balanced diet, one that enjoys the commotion of kids but also rests in moments of quiet.

⏲ TIME FOR TEACHING ⏲

Read: Psalm 23:2, Mark 6:31, and Zephaniah 3:17

Stop, drop, and breathe! Enjoy the quiet. Because taking time for peace, helps you enjoy giving away the pieces.

DAY 4

Lasting Value

The grass withers and the flowers fall but the word of our God stands forever. Isaiah 40:8

Lasting value seems to be a commodity that is forever beyond a mother's grasp. We strive for it, we dream of it, but just as a mid-life mother of four can't quite fit into her pre-children size eight jeans; it continually seems just beyond our reach. (Now, I do realize there are some size eight Moms out there. Sadly, I am just not one of them—anymore!)

Our lives are consumed with tasks that must be repeated over and over again, leaving us forever feeling undone. Just today, I believe I changed close to a dozen dirty diapers. (My one-year-old is going through a nasty bought of diarrhea.) The last diaper I changed leaked out and ran down my leg before we made it to our changing station. I guess that just means more laundry for Mom.

Speaking of laundry, I believe it ranks at the top of the charts of redundant duties. A friend once triumphantly shared that she actually succeeded in washing, folding, and putting all of the clothes away for one day. Oh how I envied her empty baskets. But, as we all know, the lasting value of that feat was short-lived.

Genesis 2:7 reads, "the Lord God formed the man from the dust of the ground…" Man was made from dust—but not woman. She was made from the man's rib. So why is it that since the beginning of time this *dust* issue has been delegated to women? Couldn't God have just made man and then commanded, "Dust—be gone!" or at least assigned the dusting duties to the man of the house. Since man was created from the tiny particles, couldn't he by chance comprehend their nature a bit better?

Please don't misunderstand my next comment. I don't want to make light of what Christ did on the cross. But, His final words have a certain appeal that I desperately yearn for. It is my dream to one day stand on top of my sparkling kitchen table surrounding by an immaculately ordered home and shout from the top of my lungs, "It is finished!" (And then have it stay that way!)

Last week I decided that for one day I would only do tasks that had lasting value. My plan was to sew and hang new curtains for my dining room windows to replace the ones that had faded terribly from the afternoon sun. As I stepped back to admire my finished product, the thought occurred to me that although my masterpiece would last more than a day, they too would eventually fade over time and once again need to be replaced. Lasting value, it continually eludes.

Walking into my kitchen I noticed that my once beautiful surprise bouquet from my husband was now too fading fast. Petals that once radiated in vibrant color now were crinkled and brown and many had given up all hope, fell from their stems, and now sadly lay strewn on my kitchen counter. As I began to lay them to rest in the garbage can, I was reminded of a memory verse my daughter and I had been studying. Isaiah 40:8 reads, "The grass withers and the flowers fall but the word of our God stands forever."

The phrase, "stands forever" lingered in my thoughts. At last, something with lasting value: the Word of God. It was here before creation and will be with us forever. Accepting its truth brings eternal life. What can be more lasting then that?

Things of this world are fleeting. Many tasks will seem forever undone but the Word of God is done, it is complete, and it has lasting value. Time spent in the Word is never wasted. It is continually refreshing and always offers new insight.

Although a Mother's work is never done, there is something that is. God's Word has lasting value and sharing it with my family and friends is something that will last forever.

☺ TIME FOR HIM ☺
Thank You, Lord for giving us Your Word. Create in me a passion for it. Use it to speak to me in a way that rejuvenates my weary soul.

Even though my Mothering tasks may forever be undone, I still feel complete knowing that You are forever by my side.

☼ TIME FOR MOM ☼

Don't you just wish that for one day things would stay done? Just last night, I told my daughter she couldn't eat ice cream for an evening snack because the kitchen was already clean and I just couldn't handle one more dirty dish. The undone-ness of Motherhood is one of my biggest frustrations. I desperately seek something to hold onto, something to stay clean... something to last more than a few minutes.

God's Word is something that you can grasp, sink your teeth into, and not feel as if you've wasted your time reading it. It is not like the latest fiction novel or even the newspaper. God's Word is everlasting.

Teaching your kid's to live by God's standard has eternal worth. Things of this world fade. Bringing others to Christ; that, my friends, has lasting value.

So, even though your to-do list beckons you during those few free minutes nap time offers. Today, lay the dust rag aside and open up your Bible. Allow God's Word to breathe life into your weary soul. Go ahead. Pour yourself a cup of coffee (or tea if you prefer), sit back and open *the* book. God has a lot he wants to say to you. Turn the pages and enjoy a lasting value far beyond laundry and dishes, a lasting value that quenches your thirsty soul and invigorates your worn out spirit.

☼ TIME FOR TEACHING ☼
Read: Psalm 119:89, Ecclesiastes 3:14, and Matthew 24:35
God's Word has lasting value. Read it.

DAY 5

Wrestling Matches

Serve wholeheartedly, as if you were serving the Lord, not men.
Ephesians 6:7

"Joseph, hold still!" I exclaimed pinning down his mid-drift with the weight of my arm as I struggled to single-handedly dismantle the soiled diaper and replace it with a clean one.

Changing this child is like wrestling an alligator. Not that I have ever actually wrestled one. Even so, I believe a parallel still exists. Joseph is strong and vivacious. He wiggles considerable. It takes all my strength to pin him down. And then there's the danger element. He's a boy. Need I say more?

Wrestling with Joseph reminded me of another wrestling match of sorts. My husband suggested that I take some food over to a sick neighbor on Monday. Today was Wednesday and I still hadn't gotten up the gumption to do it. It's not that I didn't want to see her. It was preparing the food, loading up four raga-muffin kids into our van, and then keeping them from ransacking her house while we visited. To me, it just felt like one more alligator to wrestle and I was already all wrestled out.

Wrestling matches: times that God prompts us to do acts of service that for some reason, we don't want to take the time to do. Wrestling matches come in all shapes and sizes. Often, it is the little things, like cooking a meal for a friend in need, making that phone call, or visiting a new neighbor that we wrestle with the most. God prompts us to serve Him through these tiny acts of service. Often we shrug it off, pass the buck, or claim, "That's just not my gift!" Well ladies, I hate to burst your holy bubble, but you don't always have to have *a gift* to serve. Sometimes all God needs are hands and feet and as long as you got 'em, He can use 'em.

Even so, right now, I feel the heavy sigh of your burden. I know today's Moms are overloaded enough. All of our time, and I do mean all, every second of every day, seems to be consumed with service. You may be thinking, "How can I do one more thing? I am serviced out. Service station closed!" That, my friends, is between you and God. Sometimes we do need a break. This whole book centers on the notion of taking time-out. I believe I have grasped that concept. Yet, the simple truth remains; God calls us to serve and serve we must.

The funny thing about service is that when you do it with a heart for God, burden does not become a part of that equation. Service is a joy, a privilege, a blessing to all parties involved. That's it. Service is a party of the heart and everyone is invited.

I love how Lisa Whelchel clarifies this concept in her book *Creative Correction*. She explains that service is another one of "God's Topsy-Turvy Truths."[8] On the surface it doesn't make any sense. Matthew 20:26 reads, "...whoever wants to become great among you must be your servant." Now, how in the world does that add up? But, it does, my friends, it does. And the dividends of such service, well, they are enormous. Just check out the rest of my story.

Although, I never made a meal, we did visit our neighbor with a few cookies, a card, and plenty of perky smiles from my kids. Not only did we have a great time, we came home with *more* cookies than we left with! Now, how's that for dividends of blessing!

Don't wrestle with God. Submit to His leading. Serve out of the overflow of your heart and you'll never have to close your service station.

☺ TIME FOR HIM ☺

Lord, forgive me. Sometimes the selfishness in my heart seems to be the only thing overflowing. Help me to realize that You are the great giver of time. When You call, I need take the time and put Your purposes ahead of my own. Use me to serve You by serving others.

☺ TIME FOR MOM ☺

Some time ago I had arrived at a place were I was simply serviced out. Give, give, give! That's all I ever did. The only party that resulted from my laborious efforts was a pity party with only one invitation! No one ever appreciated my wonderful acts of service. In fact, once I put together the perfect gift basket, only for my friend to not even bother to say "thank you." How do you like that!

When my son was born, I selfishly prayed that for once someone would remember me. Well, God answered that pray in a way that brought me to my knees. My friend, Gail, not only arranged for multiple meals to be brought to my home, she also organized a frozen food shower. She came to visit bearing gifts of diapers and even candy for my older kids. I was overwhelmed. Even now, years later, her awesome act of service brings tears to my eyes.

Not only did God provide for my need, He also taught me a lesson. Although I had been serving the Lord, the intent of my service always seemed to point in instead of up. I wanted the recognition! I grew to understand that when you serve with a heart for God, it doesn't matter if someone says "thank you." True service, the kind of humble service that Jesus was talking about in that verse I quoted, always points up. It always points to God. And the party it produces is always a party of praise, praise that points up, not to self.

So Mom, the ball is now in your court. (Oops! I guess that's basketball and not wrestling. Sport's lingo is obviously beyond my parameters of understanding.) Mom, what is God calling you to do? What act of service has He whispered in your ear and you've pretended to not hear. (Don't you hate when kids do this. *You heard me! Now go clean your room!*) Maybe He's calling you to make a meal for that new Mom, accept a position at church, or just offer to baby-sit for a frazzled friend. Whatever the call, don't wrestle with God. Do it. Do it with an attitude that points up and a party where everyone is invited.

⏱ TIME FOR TEACHING ⏱
Read: John 13:13-17, 1 Peter 4:9-11, and Acts 20:35
Jesus showed us how we should serve. Now it is up to us to live by His example.

Pursue the Dream

*I press on toward the goal to win the prize for which God has called
me heavenward in Christ Jesus.* Philippians 3:14

The dream, we all have one. Even you Mom! The question is
what is your dream and are you taking steps to pursue it?
I have a little photo album that reads, "Dream. Those that
reach touch the stars." How true; you can't touch until you first
reach. Reaching takes courage, risk, and reliance. We need to
courageously pursue the dream, risking it all, while continually
relying on the leadership and direction of God, the dream giver.

Following my dreams has been my lifeline and favorite time-
out activity. Although I relish Motherhood and all that it entails.
(Well, maybe not *all* of it.) I knew from the start that there was
a *more that Mommy* in me that needed to be explored. So, I have
pursued it, baby step at a time, holding back when appropriate,
and stepping forward when time allowed.

Pursuing that dream has given me a sense of identity. Although I hate to admit it, to most of the world I am known as
Joseph's Mom or Michaela's Mom or... Rarely am I called by
my actually first name. (Isn't this true? Think of some of your
acquaintances—do you know their first names?) Following my
dreams, in a sense, gives me back my name, my real name, which
is Judy Crawford if you haven't got that by now. My dream is the
part of me that isn't directly tied to the care and well being of
my family

With that said, there needs to be a word of warning. Dreams
do need to be kept in check. When kids are little, their care should
be your priority. You don't want the authorities showing up and
charging you with child neglect. Trust me, it can happen. By the
same token, that doesn't mean you should chuck your dreams that
were and still are a part of your genetic make up. During this season identify and take baby steps to pursue your dream.

TIME-OUT TIPS

Identify the dream! What gets your blood pumping? Do you want to start a business and be an entrepreneur? Or maybe be an artist and paint works of art? Why not take an accounting class and do your own taxes. Or learn gourmet cooking just for fun. The opportunities are endless... Dreams don't always have to be huge things, think big and small. Journal your thoughts, pray about it, identify some goals, and make plans to put your feet to the pavement.

Take inventory! Knowing your qualifications helps you identify the dream. Take inventory of your talents, your past successes, and your passion. Taking stock of these three areas will give you the tools and point you in the right direction.

Research! Find out what it takes to live out your dream. Read books. Educate yourself. Volunteer in your area of interest. Make connections. Locate people that are living your dream and quiz them on how they got there.

Start! This is the hardest part. Because there will always be things to do, places to go, appointments to keep. But start anyway. Set some goals and begin taking steps towards achieving them. When kids are young, you may not be able to do it all. But that's perfectly all right. Create a momentum so that when the time is right you can take that giant step forward to truly live the dream.

Pray for open doors! I have discovered that God will only open doors in His time and not any sooner. Until then, you need to trust God's timing and continue to pray.

But, I'm living the dream! For some of you, your dream is to be a wife and mother and you are living out that dream right now. I applaud you! Be the best Mom you can be and then use your talents to mentor other Moms. Or use your abilities to Mother other children. Help out in the church nursery. Become a child care volunteer at a Mom's group. Share your gift of Mothering to reach beyond the scope of your immediate family to world around you.

Before I close this section I would like to recommend a couple of books that have helped me pursue my dreams. *The Dream*

Giver by Bruce Wilkinson[9] and *The Cure for the Common Life* by Max Lucado[10]. Both are wonderful resources that I believe will lead you in the right direction.

Our children need to see Mommy dream. They need to watch us reach beyond ourselves to answer the call that God has placed on our lives. Doing so, set's a powerful example. Hopefully by observing Mom reach for the stars they in turn will reach as well. This week take time-out to dream. You are a woman with original ideas and talents that God can use to be a wonderful Mom and so much more. Cultivate your talents and pursue your dream.

A Perfect Fit

*"For I know the plans I have for you," declares the Lord, "Plans to
prosper you and not to harm you, plans to give you hope and a future."*
Jeremiah 29:11

The tug of the covers aroused my slumber as my little guy
still half asleep nestled up beside me. A quick turn of my head
caught the amber illumination from the nightstand. 3:24 glowed
in the grey night. My grogginess slowly sharpened as the meaning behind the numbers began to register. I guess my nighttime
intruder wanted a little company.

Although the *family bed* may be status quo in many of today's homes, it is an infrequent occurrence in ours. Joseph, to my
disappointment, has never been much of a cuddlier. Sneaking
in bed with Mom was a coveted treat that I relished not often
enough. I also realized that the gap was quickly closing on these
special bonding moments. Joseph, now 4 ½ was my youngest of
four children. Soon he would be running off to kindergarten and
cuddling with Mom would be permanently checked off the to-
do list of a big boy. That thought made this unexpected snuggle
even sweeter.

As he nuzzled his weary head on my chest my arm wrapped
around his slight form pulling him close. As we cuddled in the
peaceful quiet of the night, the warmth of his body triggered a
nostalgic flow as thoughts of my years of Mothering paraded
before me.

Abandoning a career in teaching, God's call to raise four
children has kept me at-home for over ten years. But soon that
would all be changing. The foreboding Kindergarten loomed in
the near future and the pre-K panic had already set in. Friends
had already succumbed to the pressure, accepting jobs while their
youngest spent his last year in daycare. I resisted that thought. I
wanted this final year. In fact, I didn't want it to end.

But still, reality would soon be here and choices would have to be made? What would I do when Joseph started school? Over the years, teaching had somehow lost its appeal leaving me at a loss to what my next career move should be. Besides, what was I qualified for anymore anyway? Years of changing diapers, a steady diet of *Land before Time* videos and an inclination to end every other word with a long "e" (potty, nappy, blank-ee…remember…) has somehow left me feeling not quite marketable in the real world. So, where do I fit? What will my next job title be when stay-at-home Mommy is no longer needed?

As these rumblings pondered in my mind, Joseph's arm reached up as if he were unconsciously attempting to raise his hand in answer to my queries. As his hand gently came to rest on my cheek, I laid the flat of my palm against his and his little fingers instinctually wrapped themselves around my index finger. At that moment an unexpected rush of hot emotion rose within as the answer to my quandary became crystal clear. I may not know what the future holds, but I do know who holds the future. As long as I wrap myself around the comfort of God's strong hand, He will lead me to my purpose, my perfect fit in the future that lies ahead.

Tears began to flow as I thanked God for my family and His years of provision so that I could stay-at-home with my kids. On and on I whispered midnight prayers of gratitude and then symbolically placed my life into His strong hands, asking God to bless my final months with my son and open doors for the future.

The gentle breeze from the rhythmic flow of the ceiling fan dried my tears while tenderly lulling me back to sleep. Sandwiched between the strong warmth of my husband on one side and my little guy tucked close to the other; their reassuring touch calmed my spirit as my breathing slowed to a steady tandem with theirs. Tomorrow will be here soon enough. For now I believe I had found my fit—the most perfect fit of all.

TIME FOR HIM

Dear Lord, You have a perfect fit for my life. For now that fit is taking care of young ones. Guide me towards the future as I trust You and boldly step forward.

⏰ TIME FOR MOM ⏰

The intense heat had taken its toll. One more thrill, one more ride until we headed home. The scrambler seemed like a logical choice. The line was short, the breeze inviting. Buckling in for our last round of fun, I teased my son as the ride jerked forward into its steady circular motion.

"Scream when I count to three," vibrated over the loudspeaker as we all gingerly complied. As we cheered each spin I noticed something peculiar. All the other workers at the park seemed to grin and bear it, exhausted from the heat, just trying to get through the day. Who could blame them? Not this worker, she dared to be different. The inviting breeze wasn't the only breath of fresh air on the scrambler that day; it was in her voice, the way she coached us to have more fun, as if it were her first experience with the ride herself.

Max Lucado calls it the *sweet spot*. It is when you "use your uniqueness to make a big deal out of God everyday of your life."[11] As Lucado's book title explains, it is the *Cure for the Common Life*, your perfect fit, God has already equipped and prepared in advance for you to do.

Mom, did you know that God has a sweet spot in mind for you? Have you found your perfect fit? Today, take inventory of your talents and experiences. What flips your switch and lights your fire? No, I am not talking about that taxing toddler pushing your buttons all day long. What excites you so much that you lose sleep at night just thinking about it. That is your sweet spot, your perfect fit, your divine purpose in life. Now that you've found it, live it! Because living out your perfect fit is the greatest thrill ride of them all.

⏰ TIME FOR TEACHING ⏰

Read: 1 Corinthians 9:24, Jeremiah 1:5 and John 15:16
How do you find your perfect fit? Read God's reassuring Words and discover His perfect fit for your life.

DAY 2

Are You a Play Dough Mom?

"Come, follow me," Jesus said, "and I will make you fishers of men."
At once they left their nets and followed him.
Matthew 4:19-20

"Mom, can we play with play dough?" my kids earnestly pleaded.

"Play dough," I murmured under my breath, "I hate play dough!"

I never could understand how a substance that by nature is supposed to stick together can break into so many tiny little pieces. Specks of brightly colored sticky stuff always end up on the floor and then little feet track it onto the carpet. I end up finding play dough for weeks hidden in places I never dreamed. *So, what should I do? Do I risk it?*

I don't know, maybe I was just experiencing a moment of weakness, but with a heavy sigh, I reluctantly relinquished, "Sure."

"All right!" my kids cheered and off they went. Soon my kitchen table was covered with pretend cookies, little plastic people with colorfully decorated spaghetti hair and yes, tiny primary colored flecks all over my pristine floor. (O.K. *pristine* might be an overstatement; how about clean enough.) Play dough. What fun!?

Basically, there are two different types of Moms: the daring fun play dough Moms and the play it safe control freak Moms. I guess I fall into the latter category. Play dough Moms love creativity. They are natural born risk takers. Potential mess yields no red flag warning to them. In fact, some of these Moms even make their own play dough from scratch. I've tried that once…once!

Then there's the boring, keep it clean because it took me forever to get it clean in the first place Moms. Which I have to admit, I am one of them! We reluctantly allow our kids any latitude with markers, finger-paints, and heaven forbid play dough. Why? Isn't it obvious? We want to keep our homes presentable. Is that really so terrible? Please, take a moment to feel my pain.

I know...I know we *are* a little too uptight. Sometimes, we need to let it go and have fun!?

Which type of Mom are you? Recall the last time your child asked you to finger paint. Did you instinctively say, "Yes!" or did you sit on the fence of decision contemplating the cost. Be honest now.

Risk taking, it's natural for colorful play dough Moms. In fact, right now they are wondering, "What's the big deal?" Play it safe Moms, well, we see things from a different pastel perspective. Let's put it this way, risk taking is one bridge we would rather not cross.

But, I believe God calls us to be risk takers, play dough Moms of sorts. Every day He stretches us to reach beyond our safe little play pens of comfort. We need to risk rejection and call up the new Mom and invite her and her kids over for a playtime. We need to risk embarrassment and take our kids to church even if they behave poorly in the pews. Finally, we need to risk it all and say yes to whatever God sized task He is prompting us to do—even when we don't feel qualified.

Risk, it's easy for some, hard for others, but necessary to truly experience the fullness of God's touch on our lives.

My kids had so much fun today; maybe I need to rethink my disgust for play dough. Maybe I need to be a play dough Mom more often. Believe it or not, I discovered that play dough does come out of carpets a little easier than I thought.

So, what do you think? Are you a play dough Mom? If you are, can my kids come over and play at your house some time?

☉ TIME FOR HIM ☉

Dear Lord, help me to be a play dough Mom. Help me to be a Mom that is willing to risk a mess to cultivate creative fun and a woman who is willing to say yes when You call me to do something that stretches me beyond my comfort level.

☉ TIME FOR MOM ☉

Are you a play dough Mom? God doesn't want us to play it safe forever. He wants us to step out in faith and reach the world for Him.

When Jesus said to the young fishermen tending their nets, "Come follow me," they had a choice. They could step out and risk everything or play it safe and keep on fishing. They did choose to keep on fishing, only instead of fishing for fish, they followed Him and became fishers of men.

I believe that right now God is asking you to step out of your boat. Think about it.

Yesterday, I signed the contract to publish this book. After the initial elation, a wave of fear swept over me and now hovers like a heavy fog of uncertainty. I didn't just step out of the boat, I jumped off the Titanic. What was I thinking! *Will this book sell? Is my writing worth the paper it's printed on? Will Moms be touched or turned off by my stories?* On and on my *play it safe* insecurities loom before me as I boldly jump ship hand in hand with the One who has called me.

I believe this is the time to send my subliminal messages. *Buy many copies of this book. Give them to your friends. Invite Judy to speak at your women's event.* Enough said.

What is God calling you to do? More importantly, what is your answer?

So, here we are again sitting on the fence of decision? Do you want to be an adventurous play dough Mom? Or do you want to play it safe and possibly miss all the joy God has in store for you?

Remember, after a period of time play dough that isn't played with becomes crusty and useless. If you continue to say no to the tasks God calls you to accomplish, your heart will eventually harden towards Him. So go ahead, *buy the book, give them to your friends*...sorry, I couldn't resist! I mean, be a play dough Mom. Accept the challenge and enjoy the thrilling journey that awaits you.

⏰ TIME FOR TEACHING ⏰
Read: Genesis 6:13-14, 22, Genesis 12:1 and 4,
and Exodus 4:10-12
The Bible is full of play dough people, men and women who took a chance and stepped out in faith. So, what do you choose?

DAY 3

Did You Know That...

A word aptly spoken is like apples of gold in settings of silver.
Proverbs 25:11

Locking eyes with my sandy blonde son, I hesitated making sure I had his full attention before posing the question. But, before I could even breathe life into the words, my son, with great delight giggled his quick response, "I know what you're going to say Mom!"

Pulling him into a head lock, I ruffled his hair with an affectionate *noogey* which lead to a great big bear hug that lifted him off the ground. *He got it,* I thought to myself, *finally, he got it.*

He didn't always get it! In fact, a few months ago he didn't *get it* at all. At the time, well, how do I politely put it, we did not get along very well. You've heard the phrase oil and water don't mix. Well our relationship best resembled the Exxon Valdez oil spill, pretty much a natural disaster. Everything he did stomped on my nerves and everything I did stomped on his self esteem. Through it all, I felt God's gentle tap of warning on my shoulder, "Judy, if you don't get a handle on your badgering, someday, you will turn this child away."

A pattern had been set. Although he complied with my demands, the hostility in his eyes told a different story. My friend, Denise, came up with a term that fit my son to the "T." He was what she called "Passive/Rebellious." That's when your child is outwardly obedient while the boiling waters of belligerence simmer just beneath the surface. It's kind of like a volcano: beautiful and serene on the outside, but on the inside, the volcanic lava of resentment festers, waiting for the right moment to erupt.

Although he had not exploded yet, I knew if things didn't change and change soon, that time would come.

So, I decided to ask the question, the simple question that created a U-turn in our relationship, the one question that says it all, "Son, do you know that I'm proud of you?"

At first his response was, "No!" Now that hurt!

So I'd ask again. Then his response was, "Kinda." This was a little better, but not there yet.

So then I'd ask again and again. Until finally he relinquished with an affirmative "Yes Mom, I know you are proud of me."

Our little conversation is somewhat reminiscent of Peter's experience in the Bible. Three times Jesus asked him, "Do you love me?" Three times Peter replied. Until finally the point was made, the commitment cemented.

Our children need to know that we love them. They need to know that we are proud of them. They say actions speak louder than words, yet still, they need to hear the words.

So, today I thought I would try again with a slightly different approach.

"Son, do you know that I *like* you?" I questioned awaiting his response.

"No!" He replied with a smirk that said it all.

Reaching forward to head lock him again, I couldn't help but smile to myself. *He gets it. But even still, maybe he needs to hear it again.*

⏰ TIME FOR HIM ⏰

Thank You, Lord, for the reminder that sometimes my words speak just as loud as my actions. Help me to always have a positive word of praise for my children and anyone else that needs to hear it. I pray that my words and actions might always be pleasing to You.

⏰ TIME FOR MOM ⏰

Do your kids know that you love them? Have you specifically told them how proud you are of them lately? We all need to hear these words on a regular basis in as many ways as they can possibly be expressed.

Gary Chapman and Ross Campbell highlight "The Five Love Languages of Children," in their book by the same title. The five languages are "Physical Touch, Words of Affirmation, Quality

Time, Gifts, and Acts of Service."[12] We each perceive love differently. If you understand your child's strongest love language you can better express your love to them in a deeper more meaningful way. Be that as it may, however you express it; the most important point is that your children know you love them.

There's a story I heard once that I believe best illustrates this point. It goes something like this...

Every night a Mother and her son played a game called *I love you more*. As the Mom tucked her son into bed, they each tried to out due the other with some illustration that best pictured the extent of their love. One night the Mom triumphantly entered her son's room determined that she would finally top them all. With a note of confidence she remarked to her son, "I love you so much, I carried you in my belly for nine long months. You can't beat that!"

The light in her son's eyes softened as he shared his reply, "But Mom, I carry you in my heart—every day."

Mom, every day you hold your child's fragile heart in your hand. Every day you have a choice. You can choose to crush that heart with constant criticism or you can choose to caress it with words of affirmation and praise.

Encourage your child. Tell him you love him. Show her you love her. Pour out your love to your child every way you can and cement the bonds of love in the heart of your child forever.

⏲ TIME FOR TEACHING ⏲
Read: Proverbs 16:24, and Hebrews 3:13
Your words have the power to build up or tear down. Today, do a little building.

DAY 4

Stuck For a Season

There is a time for everything, and a season for every activity under heaven;...a time to embrace and a time to refrain..."
Ecclesiastes 3:1, 5

Like many homes, our front door is comprised of a combination of two doors: an interior pine storm door and an exterior glassed screen door. When the kids are due home from school, I often open up the inside door so they can easily enter on their own.

Today was one such occasion. But now evening was approaching and the kids were all home from school, so it made sense to close and lock the interior wood door. With a quick turn, I pushed the door shut and then gently gave it a little push to ensure that it was latched and secure. As I began to step away, I noticed the room seemed oddly quiet, the kind of quiet that sends a Mom into an *All Points Bulletin* state of panic.

As I rapidly scanned the room for any signs of life, a strange sixth sense intuition whispered in my ear, *Open the door. That's weird.* I questioned a bit perplexed, *I just shut it, why would I need to open it back up.* But, never being one to question a Mom's odd instinctual leanings, I quickly complied with a shrug and the thought. *I guess it couldn't hurt?*

Would you know it, as soon as I opened the door, out popped my slightly smashed toddler. With a new found freedom, he quickly scampered off no worse for the wear. Wow! That sure shocked the dickens out of me. *How did he get stuck in there?* I thought quite puzzled.

As I looked out the window chuckling to myself at my son's silly pranks, I was struck with a moment of melancholy. As an at-home Mom, I often feel stuck as well. I have so many dreams, aspirations, and career goals I would love to pursue. But, for this season of time, while little feet still dash about, I am called to refrain, stuck if you will.

It's easy to feel stuck when you are an at-home Mom. In fact, I believe stuck is part of the job description. Just last week I needed to cut out the gum that was stuck in my son's hair. Every time I dare tread in front of the refrigerator, prying my feet off its sticky surface is like trekking through three feet of snow. And then there's that unidentifiable sticky goop I found at the bottom of my purse. For Moms, stuck is a way of life.

But, the worst stuck of all is the feeling that I am wasting away. Wasn't I meant to do something more, something different…something not sticky.

The feelings I have are not uncommon. Abraham was stuck without a son for years before his dream was granted. How long was David stuck lurking around in caves before he actually took the throne? Moses was stuck in the desert for forty years and just as he was about to step foot into the promised land, God passed his dream onto another. Over and over the Bible is chucked full of examples of lives that were stuck; forced to wait; caught between the promise of a dream and the gift of living it out.

As I stood there looking out my glassed door visualizing my life beyond spit up and diapers; (and believe me it was looking pretty good!) my focus shifted from the view outside my home to the smudges of tiny hand prints that littered my window.

On second thought, maybe stuck isn't such a bad place to be. Where else can I look like a train wreck (on a bad day it happens) and still enjoy sticky finger hugs that melt my heart like chocolate on a hot summer day? (Hey, maybe that's the unidentifiable at the bottom of my purse.) Where else can I cozy up with my little guy and still check it off my list of accomplishments for the day? In pursuit of my dream, I know I would miss that.

Looking out the window I noticed that overnight the tree that once danced with vibrant fall colors is not all but bare. Seasons change. Soon enough this robust season of stickiness will shift into another season of empty laps and clean kitchen floors. I know God has called me to fill this particular purpose at this particular time. For now I need to stick with it and enjoy the season.

⏲ TIME FOR HIM ⏲

Dear Lord, You have a master plan for my life and that includes the now. Dreams for the future can wait until the right time. Give me a heart that lives in the present and embraces every season of life.

⏲ TIME FOR MOM ⏲

Do you feel stuck? Maybe your kids are grown and your season of stuck is now caring for an elderly parent. Maybe you feel stuck in a job and long to be able to stay at-home. Maybe your desire is to have another child but for whatever reason God is not granting you a pink stripe on that pregnancy test.

Stuck is a feeling we all have at one time or another. It is when the grass seems greener on the other side of the fence. It is when you have a dream that for whatever reason, you need to let go of for a time to attend to matters at hand. These are all seasons of life, times God uses to develop our character, encourage us to depend on Him, and prepare us for the promised dream.

Whatever season of stuck you may be in at the moment, try to take your eyes off of the future and live in the present. We only have today—one minute—one second at a time. Wouldn't it be a shame to miss out on the sweetness of now because of a longing for tomorrow? Don't forget your dream. God placed that dream in your heart for a reason. Just don't miss the now because of a hope for tomorrow. Time is a fleeting gift that can only be lived once. Savor it. Today love the season.

⏲ TIME FOR TEACHING ⏲

Read: Psalm 39:4-5, Psalm 16:5-6, and Daniel 2:21
God has a plan for your life and it includes the now.

Unforgettable

Sarah said, "God has brought me laughter, and everyone who hears about this will laugh with me." Genesis 21:6

It was a beautiful, warm summer evening, the kind of night that was perfect for catching fireflies, playing flashlight tag in the dark, and gathering around a blazing backyard bonfire. That's exactly what we were doing. It was my turn to host the yearly family reunion. To celebrate our final evening together, all thirty-something of us (Yes, we are very fertile folk) gathered around our cozy campfire, enjoying the night air, the close bond of family, and a few good ghost stories. Each of the cousins took turns weaving their spontaneous wacky tales while sitting in the hot seat, the lawn chair closest to the fire.

Blake's tale went something like this… "The swamp air was so thick you could cut it with a knife. The boys got into the boat determined to locate the origins of the mysterious noise beckoning them in the darkness. As they drifted out into the middle of the lake, the oar from the boat crashed onto something hard in the water. Startled, the boys bravely leaned forward as a red cooler bobbed to the surface."

"Cooler!" I chortled unable to contain myself, "We found it! There's the missing cooler!" Unknowingly my nephew's pun ignited a contagious roll of laughter cementing the memory in our hearts and minds forever.

Don't you get it! We found the cooler! Well, let's take a step back in time so you can *get it* too!

The day before, it was my job along with my coerced brother-in-law to fetch ice for the coolers. When you have thirty-some odd folk to feed and keep cool in the heat of a Missouri summer, it takes a lot of ice. Hunting down every available cooler, we packed them into the back of my husband's past-its-prime pickup truck. The tailgate was missing, but that didn't seem to be a concern, we were only going a few miles.

Hunkering down the blacktop, (That's what you do in a rusty red pickup out in the country) we got our load of ice and started to make our way back. Unloading the coolers into the garage, I quickly noticed something awry. *Where is the red cooler? My brother's borrowed red cooler to be more specific.* I questioned inspecting every inch of the dusty old truck bed. (Remember, it was a farm truck with years of farm things still onboard in the back.) *Had we left it behind?* I thought mentally retracing our steps. Panic stricken, we both plopped back into cab. A cloud of dust puffed from the grimy upholster, adding irritation to our already sweaty brows. Shifting into gear, we burned a little rubber (that was all that was left on that old truck) as we set off down the country roads with high hopes of finding our misplaced cooler. Would you know it? It was gone! Gone like the cloud of dust trailing behind us! We couldn't find it on the main road...we hadn't left it behind when we got the ice...it had vanished... completely...poof! The old pickup truck backfired, adding exclamation to our dread as we rolled into the gravel drive. How we ever lost a cooler from Hatton (our neighboring community) to home still remains a mystery. But we did and now we needed to face the music which I believe was to the tune of a sad slow country ballad. Something about rusty old pickup trucks, dusty country roads, and a cooler with a mind of its own.

Returning with puppy dog tails tucked tightly behind we sang a few bars of that sorry old country song only instead of passing the buck and blaming it on the truck, we stood our ground hoping humor would be found. (Not bad. Huh! Nashville, here I come!)

But now gathered around the warmth of a backyard bonfire we found the missing cooler! We found it! Hurray! There it was and will always be, a forgotten cooler now an unforgettable memory that will continue to make us laugh for years to come.

☺ TIME FOR HIM ☺

Lord, thank You for the gift of laughter. I have to be honest; sometimes it is difficult to laugh when toes, particularly my toes have been stepped on. Help me to have a heart that forgives and eyes that see the humor in all things.

☺ TIME FOR MOM ☺

Humor is a gift...and a choice. You see, when we lost that cooler, my brother could have very easily made it into an *issue*. Who would blame him? It was brand new and a bargain on top of that. Anyone who has ever dealt with friends or family knows exactly what I am talking about.

Now, I know you are thinking, "But, it was just a cooler, what's the big deal?" That's exactly what issues are made of, little things blown up into big things that for whatever reason take up residence in the form of resentment in our hearts. My brother decided to be bigger than that, he traded the seeds of bitterness for the gift of humor. He chose to laugh. We need to laugh too!

I believe God has a keen sense of humor. Take Sarah for example. I think God had a hearty laugh when he placed baby Isaac into her ancient womb. (She was way too old to be birthing babies.) But God had other plans and I believe he chuckled a bit as He set those plans into motion.

Sarah had a choice too. She could have easily grown bitter for having the burden of caring for a young child placed on her weary shoulders at such an old age. Can you imagine toting around a diaper bag while receiving social security? Most of us might have had a *problem* with that. Instead, Sarah chose to laugh. In fact, the name Isaac literally means laughter. She giggled herself silly and treasured the blessing into an unforgettable in her heart. (Now I do realize that I am trying to change an adjective into a noun and my computer does not like that one bit, but please, *humor* me!)

Ladies, what are your *unforgettables?* What are your cherished humorous memories that live on in the heart of your family forever? Unforgettables are golden. They make family—family. They bond us in a brilliant sort of way leaving behind a legacy of love and laughter for generations to come.

When things go wrong, which happens often with kids, do you choose to laugh? Kids are hilarious! They really are! But you have to have eyes to see and a heart to embrace. Today, embrace the humor. Laugh! Hoop and holler! Snort! (I must confess I am a snorter!) Make each day unforgettable—memories that last a lifetime.

⏰ TIME FOR TEACHING ⏰

Read: Job 8:21 and Psalm 118:24

Go ahead. Laugh! Make each day unforgettable.

Last Minute Remarks

So is my word that goes out from my mouth: It will not return to me empty, but will accomplish what I desire and achieve the purpose for which I sent it. Isaiah 55:11

Well Moms, the clock is ticking, our time is almost up. Just as most Moms have a few last minute reminders as their children head out the door. (Do you have your lunch? Don't forget your coat! *Where are your shoes?!*) I too would like to leave you with some last minute advice. And how better to end than with one final story.

While the kids were watching TV, I headed downstairs to work on a project that involved cutting paper. As I feverishly attempted to finish before their show ended, my youngest pranced into the room wanting a piece of the action. At this point, I had created quite a little mess and as predicted his eyes brightened as he caught sight of the tantalizing colorful paper scraps that had now collected in a pile on the floor.

Unable to resist, he leaned over and began to finger each little piece contemplating just what to do with his new found prize. Grabbing a hand full he suddenly tossed them into the air, outstretched his tiny arms, and swung himself around in circles. With each fling of confetti, his face beamed upwards as he curiously questioned, "Where dit doe?" as if the colorful paper pieces should somehow still be hovering over his head.

As I marveled at my mischievous son, I couldn't help but ask myself the same question. *Joseph, where did it go? I believe it was just yesterday that I nestled you in my arms and now look at you so grown up, so independent, so full of life.*

There are moments I would like to freeze frame and keep forever just like Joseph expected that confetti to hover over his head. But as we all know, time marches on and moments like these are fleeting at best.

We celebrate our children's firsts, their first tooth, first smile, first steps. Did you ever think that there will be a last? There will be a last time you nurse your baby, a last time your son will take a nap, a last diaper to change? (Now that's a revelation!)

Did you know that there is a point when you shift from Mommy to Mom and all of the long "e" words mysteriously vanish from your child's vocabulary? There will be a last time your child will allow you to hold his hand in public or let you cuddle on the couch.

Ladies there will be a last.

The lasts are harder to mark because...you just never know; they sneak up from behind and suddenly, poof, they're gone.

If we had known, would we have held on longer, savored the moment more.

Mom, don't miss the moments! You need to take time-out. Take care of the care-giver. But don't forget to take time-out to have fun with your kids. God has given us a great gift, an awesome gift, the gift of children. Take time-out for yourself—so you can enjoy time-out with them.

Well Mom, I believe our time is up, the clock has ticked its final tick, the door is about to open. But please a few more words my computer has lots of memory.

They say Motherhood is the hardest job you will ever love. Mom, I challenge you, LOVE IT! I know that seems obvious, but the simple truth is that loving it is a choice, a choice we don't always choose to make. So Mom, I am reminding you, LOVE IT! Enjoy every part of it. Laugh and cry and live it to the fullest.

And even more important, LOVE GOD! He will hold your hand though all the ups and downs, the anguish and joy of it all. He is always just a breath away ready and willing to join you in this awesome journey. Above all else, love Him! It is my prayer that this book has nourished your soul, and caused you to love it all a bit more.

I now leave you with one last bit of encouragement.

First, you are a great Mom! I know you are thinking, "How

can you say that, we've never even met!" Well, I figure if you've made it this far into my book, you are a Mom that perseveres. Although I would love to think that every word written is literary genius. My children tell be otherwise. It takes perseverance to finish a book *and* perseverance to be a Mom. That plus your desire to connect with God on a deeper level makes you an awesome Mother. So, go ahead and own it. You *are* a great Mom! Finally, you are doing more good than you will ever possible know. Every day we toss stones into the pond of life hoping that our efforts will create some sort of ripple that touches the lives of others. Today, take a step back to "see the pond" to quote my friend Marcia and realize you are doing more good than you know. You *are* making a difference, one baby wipe at a time.

Now, go get 'em tiger! You can do it!

Ding! I believe that is our timer. Sorry Mom, our time is up!

Endnotes

1 John Newton, *Amazing Grace* (Nashville, TN: Convention Press, 1956), 188.

2 Karol Ladd, *The Power of a Positive Mom* (West Monroe, LA: Howard Publishing, 2001), 67.

3 Julie Ann Barnhill, *She's Gonna Blow: Real Help for Moms Dealing with Anger* (Eugene, Oregon: Harvest House Publishers, 2001)

4 *Webster's New World Dictionary* (New York, New York: Simon and Schuster, 1982), 462.

5 A condensed version of this devotional first appeared in the June 2004 issue of the *Hearts at Home Devotional Magazine*.

6 Henry T. Blackaby and Claude V. King, *Experiencing God: Knowing and Doing the Will of God* (Nashville, TN: Lifeway Press, 1990), inside back cover.

7 http://www.brainyquote.com/quotes/quotes/w/williampen107902.html

8 Lisa Whelchel, *Creative Correction: Extraordinary Ideas for Everyday Discipline* (Wheaton, IL: Tyndale House Publishers, 2000), 211.

9 Bruce Wilkinson, *The Dream Giver* (Oregon: Multnomah Publishers Sisters, 2003)

10 Max Lucado, *Cure for the Common Life: Living in Your Sweet Spot* (Nashville, TN: W Publishing Group, 2005)

11 Ibid., 7.

12 Gary Chapman and Ross Campbell, *The Five Love Languages of Children* (Chicago, IL: Northfield Publishinhg, 1997, 2005)

About the Author

Judy Crawford holds a Master's degree in Music Education and taught as a band director for many years. Her most cherished degree, however, is her MAMA which stands for Momma, which she has obtained from the School of Hard Knocks. It is from this experience of raising four children that she has obtained a wealth of humorous and heartwarming anecdotal stories that she loves to share.

Judy also has a great deal of experience in Women's ministries. She is the co-founder and continued coordinator of the Mom's Group called M.I.L.K. (Mothers, Infants, Little Kids). She also enjoys traveling and speaking at women's events. Her off-beat lighthearted humor and transparent honesty flows directly from her heart to the heart of her audience. She speaks on a wide variety of topics and would welcome the opportunity to present one of her messages to the women in your church or group meeting. Please feel free to e-mail her at the address below to obtain further information on how to schedule Judy to speak at your next event.

Judy and her husband, Gary, live in rural Mid-Missouri with their four children, Michaela, Adam, Will, and Joseph.

You may contact Judy Crawford at...
glcrawford@ktis.net

or visit her website at
www.judycrawfordspeaks.com